JESSE JACKSON

Still Fighting for the Dream

The History of the Civil Rights Movement

JESSE JACKSON

Still Fighting for the Dream

by **Brenda Wilkinson**

With an Introduction by
ANDREW YOUNG

Silver Burdett Press

Series Consultant: Aldon Morris

Cover and Text Design: Design Five, New York
Maps: General Cartography, Inc.
Series Editorial Supervisor: Richard G. Gallin
Series Supervision of Art and Design: Leslie Bauman
Series Editing: Agincourt Press
Developmental Editor: Della Rowland

Consultants: Jessie B. Gladden, Divisional Specialist, Office of Social Studies,
Baltimore City Schools, Baltimore, Maryland; Catherine J. Lenix-Hooker, Deputy
Chief, Schomburg Center for Research in Black Culture, New York Public
Library, New York City.

Text permissions:

From *Straight from the Heart* by Jesse L. Jackson. Copyright © 1987 by Jesse L.
Jackson. Reprinted by permission of Fortress Press.
Excerpts from *Black Women Writers* by Mari Evans, copyright © 1983 by Mari
Evans. Used by permission of Doubleday, a division of Bantam, Doubleday, Dell
Publishing Group, Inc.
Picture Credits: A/P Wide World Photos: cover background, 7, 39, 40, 50, 58, 66,
71, 86, 104, 108, 109 (top and bottom), 119; Black Star/Bob Fitch: cover portrait;
Pittsburgh Courier: 76; Schomburg Center for Research in Black Culture, N.Y.
Public Library, Astor, Lenox and Tilden Foundations: 16, 17 (top and bottom), 37,
47, 62, 63 (Laurance Henry Collection), 109 (inset); Robert Sengstacke: 87.

Library of Congress Cataloging-in-Publication Data

Wilkinson, Brenda Scott.
    Jesse Jackson: still fighting for the dream / by Brenda Wilkinson; with an
introduction by Andrew Young.
    p.   cm. —(The History of the civil rights movement)
    Includes bibliographical references and index.
    Summary: Follows the life and career of the black civil rights worker who has
twice sought a presidential nomination and continues to work for equal rights for
all Americans.
    1. Jackson, Jesse, 1941—Juvenile literature. 2. Afro-Americans—Biography—
Juvenile literature. 3. Presidential candidates—United States-Biography—Juvenile
literature. 5. Afro-Americans—Civil rights—Juvenile literature. 6. Civil rights
movements—United States—History—20th century—Juvenile literature. [1.
Jackson, Jesse, 1941- . 2. Civil rights workers. 3. Afro-Americans—Biography.] I.
Title. II. Series.
E185.97.J25W48   1990
973.927′092—dc20
973.927′092—dc20
[B]
[92]   90-32008
ISBN 0-382-09926-5 (lib bdg.)   ISBN 0-382-24064-2 (pbk.)   CIP
                                                                          AC

CONTENTS

INTRODUCTION
By Andrew Young

Some thirty years ago, a peaceful revolution took place in the United States, as African Americans sought equal rights. That revolution, which occurred between 1954 and 1968, is called the civil rights movement. Actually, African Americans have been struggling for their civil rights for as long as they have been in this country. Before the Civil War, brave abolitionists were calling out for an end to the injustice and cruelty of slavery. Even after the Civil War freed slaves, African Americans were still forced to fight other forms of racism and discrimination—segregation and prejudice. This movement still continues today as people of color battle racial hatred and economic exploitation all over the world.

The books in this series tell the stories of the lives of Ella Baker, Stokely Carmichael, Fannie Lou Hamer, Jesse Jackson, Malcolm X, Thurgood Marshall, Rosa Parks, A. Philip Randolph, and Martin Luther King, Jr.—just a few of the thousands of brave people who worked in the civil rights movement. Learning about these heroes is an important lesson in American history. They risked their homes and their jobs—and some gave their lives—to secure rights and freedoms that we now enjoy and often take for granted.

Most of us know the name of Dr. Martin Luther King, Jr., the nonviolent leader of the movement. But others who were just as important may not be as familiar. Rosa Parks insisted on her right to a seat on a public bus. Her action started a bus boycott that changed a segregation law and sparked a movement.

Ella Baker was instrumental in founding two major civil rights organizations, the Southern Christian Leadership Conference (SCLC) and the Student Nonviolent Coordinating Committee (SNCC). One of the chairpersons of SNCC, Stokely Carmichael, is perhaps best known for making the slogan "Black Power" famous. Malcolm X, the strong voice from the urban north, rose from a prison inmate to a powerful black Muslim leader.

Not many people know that the main organizer of the 1963 March on Washington was A. Philip Randolph. Younger leaders called Randolph the "father of the movement." Fannie Lou Hamer, a poor sharecropper from Mississippi, was such a powerful speaker for voters rights that President Lyndon Johnson blocked out television coverage of the 1964 Democratic National Convention to keep her off the air. Thurgood Marshall was the first African American to be made a Supreme Court justice.

Many who demanded equality paid for their actions. They were fired from their jobs, thrown out of their homes, beaten, and even killed. But they marched, went to jail, and put their lives on the line over and over again for the right to equal justice. These rights include something as simple as being able to sit and eat at a lunch counter. They include political rights such as the right to vote. They also include the equal rights to education and job opportunities that lead to economic betterment.

We are now approaching a level of democracy that allows all citizens of the United States to participate in the American dream. Jesse Jackson, for example, has pursued the dream of the highest office in this land, the president of the United States. Jackson's running for president was made possible by those who went before him. They are the people whose stories are included in this biography and history series, as well as thousands of others who remain nameless. They are people who depend upon you to carry on the dream of liberty and justice for all people of the world.

Civil Rights Movement Time Line

—1954———1955———1956———1957—

May 17—
Brown v. *Board of Education of Topeka I:* Supreme Court rules racial segregation in public is unconstitutional.

May 31—
Brown v. *Board of Education of Topeka II:* Supreme Court says desegregation of public schools must proceed "with all deliberate speed."

August 28—
14-year-old Emmett Till is killed in Money, Mississippi.

December 5, 1955–December 20, 1956—
Montgomery, Alabama bus boycott.

November 13—
Supreme Court outlaws racial segregation on Alabama's city buses.

January 10, 11—
Southern Christian Leadership Conference (SCLC) is founded.

August 29—
Civil Rights Act is passed. Among other things, it creates Civil Rights Commission to advise the president and gives government power to uphold voting rights.

September 1957–
Little Rock Central High School is desegregated.

—1962———1963———1964—

September 29—
Federal troops help integrate University of Mississippi ("Ole Miss") after two people are killed and several are injured.

April to May—
Birmingham, Alabama, demonstrations. School children join the marches.

May 20—
Supreme Court rules Birmingham's segregation laws are unconstitutional.

June 12—
NAACP worker Medgar Evers is killed in Jackson, Mississippi.

August 28—
March on Washington draws more than 250,000 people.

September 15—
Four girls are killed when a Birmingham church is bombed.

November 22—
President John F. Kennedy is killed in Dallas, Texas.

March–June—
St. Augustine, Florida, demonstrations.

June 21—
James Chaney, Michael Schwerner, and Andrew Goodman are killed while registering black voters in Mississippi.

July 2—
Civil Rights Act is passed. Among other things, it provides for equal job opportunities and gives the government power to sue to desegregate public schools and facilities.

August—
Mississippi Freedom Democratic Party (MFDP) attempts to represent Mississippi at the Democratic National Convention.

2

1958 — 1959 — 1960 — 1961

September 1958–August 1959—
Little Rock Central High School is closed because governor refuses to integrate it.

February 1—
Student sit-ins at lunch counter in Greensboro, North Carolina, begin sit-in protests all over the South.

April 17—
Student Nonviolent Coordinating Committee (SNCC) is founded.

May 6—
Civil Rights Act is passed. Among other things, it allows judges to appoint people to help blacks register to vote.

Eleven African countries win their independence.

May 4—
Freedom Rides leave Washington, D.C., and head south.

September 22—
Interstate Commerce Commission ordered to enforce desegregation laws on buses, and trains, and in travel facilities like waiting rooms, rest rooms, and restaurants.

1965 — 1966 — 1967 — 1968

January–March—
Selma, Alabama, demonstrations.

February 21—
Malcolm X is killed in New York City.

March 21–25—
More than 25,000 march from Selma to Montgomery, Alabama.

August 6—
Voting Rights Act passed.

August 11–16—
Watts riot (Los Angeles, California).

June—
James Meredith "March Against Fear" from Memphis, Tennessee, to Jackson, Mississippi. Stokely Carmichael makes slogan "Black Power" famous during march.

Fall—
Black Panther Party for Self-Defense is formed by Huey Newton and Bobby Seale in Oakland, California.

June 13—
Thurgood Marshall is appointed first African-American U.S. Supreme Court justice.

Summer—
Riots break out in 30 U.S. cities.

April 4—
Martin Luther King, Jr., is killed in Memphis, Tennessee.

April 11—
Civil Rights Act is passed. Among other things, it prohibits discrimination in selling and renting houses or apartments.

May 13–June 23—
Poor People's March: Washington, D.C., to protest poverty.

1 FROM THESE ROOTS

> **66** *I just want young Americans to do me one favor—just one favor. Exercise the right to dream.* **99**
>
> **JESSE JACKSON**

On December 19, 1988, a group of black leaders called a press conference in Chicago, Illinois.

At this meeting, the main speaker was the Reverend Jesse Louis Jackson, the first black man ever to run officially for president of the United States.

Jesse Jackson said that black people in this country should call themselves by a different name. *African American* is a better description than black, he declared.

Many words have been used in the United States to describe blacks, or African Americans. Depending on how a word is

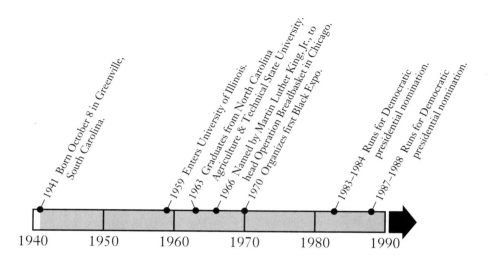

1941 Born October 8 in Greenville, South Carolina.

1959 Enters University of Illinois.

1963 Graduates from North Carolina Agriculture & Technical State University.

1966 Named by Martin Luther King, Jr., to head Operation Breadbasket in Chicago.

1970 Organizes first Black Expo.

1983–1984 Runs for Democratic presidential nomination.

1987–1988 Runs for Democratic presidential nomination.

1940   1950   1960   1970   1980   1990

used, it can be insulting or reflect pride. These words include *colored, Negro, people of color, black, Afro-American,* and *African American.*

Jesse Jackson pointed out that names used for other ethnic groups, such as Asian Americans and Italian Americans, are tied to a specific land. It gives people pride to have roots that go back into history, Jackson declared. He said that it was time for his people to claim ties to the land of their origin.

Right after Jesse Jackson gave his speech, many people, both black and white, started using the new term in day-to-day conversation. There were stories in the newspapers about the change. Discussions about it took place on television.

If just anyone had made the speech about African Americans, nothing might have happened. Newspaper reporters and television crews probably would have asked, "Who is this person who dares to speak for so many?" But the announcement did not come from just anyone; it came from Jesse Louis Jackson, one of the most famous and respected black men in America, the first African American who had a chance to be nominated for president.

Jesse Jackson earned special respect over many years. He was

Jesse Jackson in 1990 visits South Africa and speaks out against racial discrimination.

a follower of Dr. Martin Luther King, Jr. In those years, he came to be one of the most important figures in the civil rights movement. Since then, he has taken the lessons he learned from King and used them well.

Both times that he ran for president, in 1984 and 1988, Jesse Jackson made a pledge to work for the underclass. The underclass includes those who are homeless, those who are poor, and those who are uneducated. People of all races can be found in the underclass. Jesse Jackson called for changes to be made by the government so that the homeless, the poor, and the uneducated would have a better chance in life. This is why he has been described as a "friend of life's victims."

As he set out to run for president, Jesse found that many people shared his feelings about the need for major changes by the government. Here, too, were people of all races. There were red-, yellow-, white-, and black-skinned people—all believing in King's dream of justice and equality for all people. Jesse Jackson and his followers formed a group called the Rainbow Coalition. Their goal was to carry the dream forward.

Jesse's deep sense of caring about the underclass can be traced not only to the influence of Dr. Martin Luther King, Jr., but also to his childhood. He has felt driven to help oppressed people because of what he saw when he was growing up in the South. As a boy he lived under segregation laws during the 1940s and 1950s. He couldn't eat in the same restaurants whites ate in. He couldn't sit in the same part of the bus whites sat in. He couldn't even drink out of the same water fountains. So he knew from firsthand experience what it is like to be treated as a second-class citizen.

Jesse Jackson also reached out to people because he knew what it felt like to be an outsider. His mother was a teenager when he was born, and she was not married to his father. People looked down on Jesse and were cruel to him because of this. But he learned to deal with people's unkind attitudes. After he was grown, he often spoke of his origins, for he knew that if he shared the story of his beginnings, other people might find hope.

As Jackson's grandmother, Matilda Burns, might have said: It is not where a person comes from that counts, but where he or she is going.

This is the story of where Jesse Jackson came from and how he overcame the hardships of racial discrimination to run for the nation's highest office.

We all know that there are different kinds of families. In the traditional family household, there is a mother and a father, with the father acting as the head of the family. But a grandmother can also be the head of a family. Sometimes, it is a combination of mother, father, and one or more grandparents who make up what is called an extended family.

In the early years of his life, Jesse Jackson was part of an extended family. He was born on October 8, 1941, in Greenville, South Carolina. He was raised for the first two years of his life by his teenage mother, Helen Burns, and by his grandmother, Matilda Burns.

When he was two years old, Jesse's mother married Charles Henry Jackson, who legally adopted Jesse. Because Charles Jackson loved his young stepson very much and felt that Jesse was truly his own, he saw no need to tell him that he was not his natural, or birth, father. Eventually, Jesse learned the truth, but this didn't matter much in the end. What mattered was that, over the years, he received the same love as his brother Charles, the second of Helen and Charles Jackson's children.

When a teenage girl who is not married has a child, the years ahead are usually very difficult for both of them. But Jesse and his young mother were blessed, for they had help from Jesse's grandmother, Matilda, whom Jesse called Aunt Tibby.

Jesse's mother, Helen, had been an only child. People who grew up with her remember Helen Burns as a very beautiful and talented girl. She sang in the choir at school and at church. Before she learned that she was pregnant, Helen had been offered scholarships to five music schools. Sadly, her pregnancy meant that she would not be able to attend any of these schools. Instead, she stayed home to take care of her baby. This was a very big disappointment to her mother, Matilda, who had been an unmarried teenage mother herself. Matilda had worked all her life as a maid and had placed all her hopes and dreams in her daughter, Helen. Like most parents, Matilda wanted her child to have a better life than the one she had known.

But there was no time for worrying during the fall of 1941. A baby was on the way, and preparations had to begin for the birth. When baby Jesse was born, his grandmother loved him from the first moment she saw him. She did all she could to make life as comfortable as possible for her grandbaby and his mother.

Help for the new baby also came from Jesse's natural father,

Noah Robinson. Mr. Robinson lived next door, and he was married to someone else. Even though he was not married to Jesse's mother he still played an important role in Jesse's life.

In fact, Noah Robinson decided what the little boy's name would be. He said that he should have the name Jesse. Noah Robinson's father, a Baptist minister, had been named Jesse Robinson. This Jesse had a twin brother named Jacob who was also a minister. The Robinson twins were part Cherokee. Noah Robinson's mother was a former slave whose father was Irish. So Jesse Jackson, like many African Americans, has roots that trace back to a racially mixed line of ancestors.

Noah Robinson had three more sons who were born after Jesse. He named the oldest of these boys Noah, Jr. Only 10 months younger than Jesse, Noah Robinson, Jr., looked a lot like Jesse. There are many stories about how Jesse came to learn who his real father was. According to Noah, Jr., it was *his* discovery of the truth that led to Jesse's getting the facts.

Noah said that when he was around age five or six, he saw a little boy who looked very much like him. The boy was standing on the sidewalk, staring toward the house where the Robinsons lived. That boy was Jesse. As Noah stood watching the boy who looked so much like him, someone whispered to him, "See that kid over there with the curly hair? Well, he's your brother."

Noah said that at first he did not believe the story. But when he went to his father, he learned it was true. At that point, Noah, Sr., brought Jesse to the Robinson house and introduced the boys to each other as brothers. And this, Noah said, is how he came to know the truth about how he and Jesse were related.

Jesse himself, however, is convinced that this was not the first time he was told that Noah Robinson was his father. He remembers his mother showing him pictures when he was a very little boy. In these pictures, she pointed out Noah Robinson as Jesse's father. The memory of the pictures must have had its impact on Jesse. It seemed that there was something on his mind about the situation when he was a little boy. Even before he and Noah, Jr., were told that they were half brothers, Mr. Robinson recalled seeing Jesse stand and stare at the Robinson house. This was a touching sight. Mr. Robinson said that after he waved at Jesse, the boy seemed content to wave back and run on along.

Mr. Robinson later wished that he had been more involved in Jesse's life while the boy was growing up. But this had not been easy to do. His wife—Noah, Jr.'s, mother—was uncomfortable about the situation. She felt embarrassed because her husband had another child living right next door. Noah, Jr., remembered hearing his mother argue with his father about money that he gave to Jesse for special things like Easter clothes.

Mrs. Robinson was worried about all the questions that could come up between Jesse and Noah if the two children played together. Eventually, Noah was sent away from home to attend Catholic school so that the boys would be separated.

Greenville was a small town, and all the people in Jesse's neighborhood knew one another. So naturally, there was gossip among the grown-ups about Helen Burns and Noah Robinson. As a boy, Jesse no doubt heard talk about his birth many times over, from both grown-ups and children. Back then, when hardly anybody owned a television, a favorite way for older people to pass the time was to sit on each other's front porches and talk. And children loved to sit around listening, until some grown person sent them away. So Jesse had many opportunities to hear the facts.

Today we hear stories of the growing number of teenage mothers. But this was not as common when Jesse's mother was a girl. Back then, the community was much more critical of a girl in Helen Burns's situation. Pregnant girls were not permitted to return to school after they had a baby, as they are today. Helen was even asked to leave her Baptist church. She was not allowed to return until she stood before the congregation and apologized. In time, the church and the community forgave Helen Burns and Noah Robinson. But the cruel gossip did not stop.

The children in the playground teased Jesse and said mean things to him. They told him that he had no daddy and that he was a nobody. When he was a teenager, another ugly incident took place. Walking home from school one day, he heard a gossiping old woman refer to him as "Noah's bastard."

Jesse was hurt and very angry. But he remained calm. Turning to the old woman, he spoke respectfully, as he'd been trained to do by his mother and grandmother. "Go ahead," he said calmly, "call me what you will. I am Noah's bastard, if that's what you want to call me. But one day you'll be glad to know this bastard."

Jesse was determined to make this woman regret her words. Name-calling could not break his spirit or make a lesser person of him. In time he would show this old town gossip—and all the people in Greenville who thought the way she did—that he *was*, indeed, somebody.

THE OLD SOUTH

The law cannot make a man love, religion and education must do that. But it can control his efforts to lynch.

MARTIN LUTHER KING, JR.

When Jesse was a boy, 15 percent of the people in his hometown of Greenville, South Carolina, were black. The main industry there was the textile mills. Nearly all the blacks worked at the mills or had jobs in the homes of whites. The local whites owned every major business in town. The main shopping district was called Uptown. There, all the stores, restaurants—everything—were operated by whites. There were a few businesses owned by blacks, such as a cab station, a funeral home, and perhaps a café here and there. But all of these were located in the black section of town. Uptown, the *real* business section, was strictly white owned. Blacks were free to spend their money there. They were not free, however, to run any kind of store or work behind the cash registers where the goods were sold.

This was because there was separation of the races in Greenville, as throughout all of the South. When Jesse was growing up in the 1940s and 1950s, this separation was called segregation. So Jesse and other southern black children of his generation grew up as second-class citizens. The civil rights laws, which Jesse Jackson and others would later crusade for and win, had not yet been passed. Because these laws did not exist, daily life for blacks across the South was harsh and unfair.

Uptown, there were White Only signs on water fountains and at luncheon stands. Jesse's family and other blacks went shopping Uptown for clothing, food, and furniture. Jesse would often say that he didn't want to drink water because he wasn't thirsty. By pretending in this way, he and his friends didn't feel so ashamed.

In some of the stores there were water fountains labeled Colored. Seldom was the water cool at these fountains provided for blacks. At the White Only fountains, on the other hand, the water was often chilled. Jesse and his friends had to pass by those White Only water fountains, no matter how thirsty they might have been.

At the five-and-dime store, the area where blacks were allowed to eat was very different from the area reserved for whites. You would usually find some tiny hotdog stand that could seat no more than four or five people, with the Colored sign displayed. The little hotdog stand was supposed to substitute for the restaurant on the other side of the store where whites could sit and dine in style.

In many of the clothing stores, blacks were not allowed to try on clothes. And in shoe stores, black mothers learned to come prepared with their own socks. Otherwise, the shoe-store owner would pull out the dirty socks that were handed to any black person wishing to try on shoes.

Such open insults were part of everyday life in the South for young Jesse and his race. "I remember when I was in the first grade," Jesse recalled. "There were no famous black writers, no blacks on television, no black news reporters. We couldn't attend certain schools, couldn't be executives, didn't have banks....Some white people had signs on lawns that read, 'dogs and niggers keep off.' They put us down," he said.

There was separation, or segregation, in schools, churches, restaurants, and rest rooms and on public transportation. There was segregation of the races everywhere in the South.

When people say "the Old South," they are referring to the South of yesterday, the period before the late 1960s. In those years, this kind of segregation was called "Jim Crow," after a comical black minstrel show character. Under Jim Crow, blacks had to use separate entrances in movie theaters, and they could only sit in the balcony. Blacks had to sit in separate waiting rooms in bus stations. When traveling north, southern blacks were forced to sit in one car of the train. Blacks were supposed to tip their hats when they passed whites, but whites didn't even have to take off their hats when they entered a black's home.

Segregation existed in the North during this period, too. But the North had what was known as *de facto* segregation. This means that although there were no laws forcing the separation of black and white people, the separation still took place. Segregation that existed in the North was not legislated, as it was in the South. Northern segregation was not enforced by law. Segregation in the North was something practiced partly through economics. In other words, if blacks had enough money, there were restaurants they could eat in and hotels where they could stay. Most black people, however, could not afford to eat in fancy restaurants or stay in fine hotels. And there were, of course, neighborhoods where they could not afford to live. In the

We Shall Overcome

Poverty was a fact of life for many African Americans, even after slavery was ended in 1865. Slavery may have come to an end after the Civil War, but segregation, or separation, of the races did not. Segregation was even made legal by a court case decided by the U.S. Supreme Court in 1896.

Other, more violent, methods were used against African Americans. After the Civil War, white racists in the South formed the Ku Klux Klan. The KKK ever since has used a variety of methods including violent ones such as burning homes and lynching, or murdering, African Americans. But KKK members were not the only people responsible for violence against African Americans. Burnings, beatings, shootings, and lynchings were common all over the country.

Nevertheless, African Americans survived and made economic and political progress. Their rich African-American cultural heritage, the energy of black churches, and the strength of the black family helped African Americans in the hundred years after the Civil War.

For over 100 years, the Ku Klux Klan has used the burning cross to terrorize African Americans.

Women from six states picket the White House to protest violence against African Americans.

Houses like this one were the only affordable homes for many African-American families.

North, even if blacks were well off, they were still segregated. Some blacks could afford to live where they wanted. But there were unwritten laws that kept them out of certain neighborhoods. So it turned out that there were many all-black schools and many all-white schools. Public schools during the 1950s and 1960s in the North were just as segregated as Jesse Jackson's school in Greenville, South Carolina.

Blacks were not hired to work behind the cash registers in department stores in the South during this period. But few could get this kind of job in the North either before the 1960s.

So the civil rights movement, which started out to improve the lives of southern blacks, also helped those who lived in the North. Black Americans in both the South and North had fought for their country. And they had labored to help the United States become as rich as it was. They had waited long enough for their full rights as citizens.

Southern blacks never liked the rules and regulations they lived under during these years. But they had little hope that things would change. This was because the power to do anything about change did not seem to be in their hands. All of the authority to rule was in the hands of local whites. And most local white leaders were not thinking about changing anything. Whites owned almost all the businesses, had most of the good jobs, lived in the best houses, and most important, held almost all the government jobs so they could make the laws.

If new leaders had ever been voted in, change would have come. This was something that those in charge understood well. So over the years, political leaders did everything in their power to see that as few blacks as possible were able to vote.

In some southern towns, what might be called dirty tricks were played when blacks showed up to register to vote. For example, extra-hard tests were given. These were tests that whites did not have to take. Stories have even been told of how some blacks were actually given newspapers written in a foreign language and then were tested on how well they could read them. The testers would send these blacks away, telling them that they could not register to vote because they could not read.

Other stories have been told of poor blacks being given food or a few dollars to stay away from voting places. All kinds of mean tricks were used. That is why Jesse Jackson has since urged African Americans to exercise their right to vote. He remembers how intensely many people once wanted this privilege. He will never forget all the suffering and humiliation that his people went through to gain this basic freedom.

Jesse remembered one of the dirtiest tricks that was used to keep blacks from voting—the night raids of the Ku Klux Klan. The Klan was (and still is) a violent group of white racists who spread hate and fear wherever they went. Wearing masks and hooded sheets to hide their identities, they rode through the streets of black neighborhoods. They burned huge crosses and fired gunshots into the air. Blacks never knew for sure just who was hiding under the sheets. Often it was the local doctor or some person they bought goods from Uptown. Many so-called respectable white men and women were part of the Klan.

These whites did not see themselves as a hate group. In their backward way of thinking, they were protectors of their way of life. They wanted everything to remain the same as it had always been in the South. The Klan's acts of terror were their way of telling blacks to stay in their place. The Klan often went further than just threats, however. Sometimes they committed murder. At times, they thought nothing of snatching some innocent black person from a dark, deserted road and simply hanging him or her from the nearest tree. This was called lynching. You can imagine how much fear of the Ku Klux Klan there was in the Old South.

Noah Robinson, who earned a good salary at the textile mill and owned his home, was one black man who never feared the Klan or anyone else. Noah Robinson was once an amateur boxer. It was said that he had had a couple of fights with white men. "Few whites got funny with Daddy," Jesse's brother Noah, Jr., commented. He claimed his father would have "punched them out" had they bothered him.

This boldness was rare. Most black men were simply too dependent on whites for their means of survival to challenge the Southern way of life. Black children learned early on that there were rules and regulations that they, too, were expected to follow in the Old South. When Jesse was a boy, something happened that made the point clear in his mind.

Jesse and a group of his friends went to the store to buy some candy. Jesse was impatient for the grocer to take their money so that they could be on their way. So he whistled to get the store owner's attention.

Then Jesse called to him innocently. He said he needed some candy right away. The grocer became furious that a black boy had addressed him in such a casual way. The boy had spoken to him in the way that white men in the South spoke to black men. White men were always saying to black men and boys during this period, "Hey, Joe, Jim," or whatever they felt like calling them. But they did not expect blacks to talk to them in the same way. And whistling at a white man? This was unthinkable. The grocer reached beneath the counter and grabbed his gun. Then he pointed it at Jesse and told him not to whistle at a white man ever again.

No one in the store, black or white, said a word, as a trembling Jesse and his friends hurried out of the door. They ran straight home. Scenes like this one were early lessons of southern white supremacy to Jesse and his friends.

There was another time that Jesse got some idea of how black people were kept down by whites. This came during a championship boxing match that Joe Louis had with a contender. Joe Louis was an African-American boxer—one of the best fighters of all time. A group of kids were gathered in front of a cigar

store listening to the radio, Jesse recalled. Joe Louis was batter-
ing his white opponent. But Jesse said he didn't dare show any
emotion over a black man beating a white one. He knew it
would anger the white shopkeeper and his friends.

Jesse and the children he grew up with were taught in their
homes the dos and don'ts of life in the South. They learned
some of the rules along the way. There were little things, like
walking down the street and seeing a white person coming from
the other direction. The white person would hardly ever move
to the other side. Black teenagers were sometimes bold enough
to hold their ground. As a rule, however, black people always

moved over. This was a little thing. But a small incident that may have seemed only playful could cost a black child his or her very life. Black children were always warned by their parents and teachers, "Just be careful."

In 1955, a young black boy, the same age as Jesse Jackson, was visiting his relatives in Money, Mississippi. He was not aware of the danger of speaking out in front of whites. The young boy's name was Emmett Till. He was from Chicago, Illinois.

Young Emmett, along with a cousin and some other youths, went into a local store. Only 14 years old and in eighth grade, Emmett enjoyed kidding around. Flashing a photo of a white girl from back home in Chicago, Emmett bragged to the boys that this was his girlfriend. The boys, of course, told him that this would never be allowed in Mississippi.

Wanting to really shock his friends, Emmett turned as they were leaving the store and spoke casually to a white woman. "Bye, baby," he said.

The white woman felt her "southern honor" had been attacked by a black boy. So did her husband and other whites in the town.

For this remark, young Emmett was taken from his uncle's home during the night. According to reports, this is what happened next. His uncle pleaded with the white men, explaining that Emmett was not familiar with "southern ways." But the men didn't care. They drove Emmett to the Tallahatchie River and made him carry a 75-pound cotton-gin fan on his back. Emmett was ordered to take all of his clothes off. The men beat him brutally, then shot him in the head. Emmett was found three days later in the river. The cotton-gin fan was fastened around his neck with barbed wire. A bullet was in his skull, one eye was hanging out, and his forehead was crushed.

Emmett's body was so damaged that relatives could almost not identify him. *Jet*, a black magazine, ran photographs of the corpse. So did other publications and newspapers. The accused murderers of Emmett Till were brought to trial, but an all-white jury set them free.

Black children of Jesse's generation looked at the pictures of young Emmett Till over and over. They could not help thinking that this could have happened to them—any one of them.

3 COMING OF AGE

Who/can be born black/and not/sing/the wonder of it/the joy/ the/challenge

MARI EVANS, poet

When Jesse was growing up, most of his friends lived in shotgun houses. These were miserable, run-down shacks. There is a legend behind the name shotgun house. It is said that a man once stood at the front door of one of these little houses. He was able to shoot a bullet from the front door straight through to the back door. Shotgun houses had a front room, which was supposed to be a living room, but some member of the family usually slept there. Then came the middle room, where the rest of the family slept. The third and final room was the kitchen. The bathroom was on the back porch— or worse, in the backyard. Few of the shotgun houses had inside plumbing, and some had no electricity.

Some of Jesse's poorer neighbors lived in these shotgun houses. During his boyhood, he watched them dodge rent collectors when they did not have the money to pay. A Mr. Helum owned all the houses, Jesse recalled. Mr. Helum was white. He would come around some days with his account book. The people who hadn't paid their rent would often hide in the bushes and pretend not to be home. They were scared and Jesse resented that.

Jesse was fortunate that he did not live in a shotgun house. The Jackson family's standard of living was comfortable. But Jesse always found himself comparing the way they lived to the way the Robinsons lived. Charles Jackson earned a good living at the post office. Working for the post office was considered a high-income job for a black man to have. Jesse's mother added to the money coming into their home by working as a hairdresser.

Jesse and his brother, Charles, had enough clothing, food, and a roof over their heads. They lived far better than most of the children they went to school with, and they were actually envied by some.

A childhood friend who attended school in the early years with Jackson recalled that he had thought of Jesse as rich. "He was the only person I knew who had a phone in his house," said the classmate. "He did not live in the kind of shotgun house that most of us did. And Jesse was always clean!" he said of the fine clothes that Jesse would become known for in later school years.

Still Jesse did not have what Noah, Jr., and his other half brothers had. Their house and even their yard may have looked nicer. But more than material things, Jesse envied the time that Noah and his brothers had with their father. He longed to be part of the many trips his half brothers and their father took together.

Through his boss, a Mr. Ryan at the textile mill, Mr. Robinson was able to arrange for special trips north for his family. Mr. Ryan was able to get space on what was called the sleeping car of the train. This car had beds for the comfort of people who could afford them. Those who could not would have to sleep in their seats and be all worn out at the end of the trip. This was how nearly all blacks traveled. But Mr. Robinson and his family were able to pay for a sleeping car. Every summer they traveled to Philadelphia in comfort. Jesse was not a part of these trips.

Soon the Robinsons moved to the very best black section of town. Charles Jackson also moved his family to a better home, but it was not as grand as the Robinsons' home. Even the whites in town would ride past and say how fine Noah Robinson's home was! Mr. Robinson put a basketball court out back for his boys. What really made the house stand out to Jesse was the big *R* on the chimney. The *R*, for Robinson, could have stood for Jesse's name.

The hurt that Jesse may have felt led him to develop a habit of boasting as he grew up. He bragged about his clothes, about the things he was going to do, about the boyhood jobs he'd held—about everything!

The attractive suits and ties he wore to school as a teenager made him stand out. And that was just the way he wanted it! He felt he needed to prove that he was as good as, or better than, the next person.

As he got older, Jesse visited the Robinsons more often. The parents were not so worried anymore that the boys would be confused about Jesse's being their half brother. Jesse started to feel at ease in the Robinson home.

It was during one of these visits that Jesse said to his father, "Just watch. I'm going to be more than you think I can be." Jesse felt he had to prove something to everybody—including his natural father. He wanted Noah Robinson to be proud that he was his son. Mr. Robinson was indeed proud of Jesse and thought Jesse knew that. But Jesse needed even more approval.

As an adult, Jesse later said that he had been fortunate to have a second family. For there, he received additional support and encouragement as a child.

Jesse might have known comfort through his two families,

but there was much poverty around him. Daily he saw that the lives of most black children were very different from his. Besides the broken-down houses so many of them lived in, he saw children who did not get enough to eat. Jesse saw others without proper clothing to wear to school. He believed that no one should have to live this way. Jesse also saw the elderly suffer. In one of the many speeches he has given over the years, he referred to one poor old man from his hometown:

> Well, there was this old man named Mr. Davis. Mr. Davis couldn't read and write. Those days in South Carolina black people couldn't be on Welfare. Black folks didn't have any money. When they were old, they had to sit around and die. And some old, kind benevolent lady like Miss Ida would just feed them. There were two or three people in the neighborhood who just kept big pots of vegetable soup on. When folks didn't have any food they couldn't go to the Salvation Army because they were black. [The Salvation Army did not serve blacks there during this time, according to Jackson.] They couldn't get Social Security; they couldn't get on Welfare. But folks had a tradition of being kind to each other. And so, since Mr. Davis didn't have his Social Security and couldn't get on Welfare, my momma used to try to help him. She had spent several months going back and forth to try to get his Social Security and finally had to get a lawyer named John Coverson—a white lawyer, a generous man who drove Mr. Davis all the way to Washington from Greenville, South Carolina, just to try to get his Social Security.

The poverty and suffering Jesse saw among his people made him realize that something needed to be changed. And Jesse wanted to work for this change. He longed for the day when his people would be treated fairly and live more decent lives. He longed for the day when they would have greater dignity.

INFLUENCE OF CHURCH AND SCHOOL

> **❝** *I grew up a well-loved child in a loving family and so I have always known that being poor had nothing to do with lovingness or familyness or character...other people's opinions didn't influence us about that...being poor or whatever your circumstance, you are capable of being the best of people...and that best does not come from the outside in, it comes from the inside out.* **❞**

LUCILLE CLIFTON, poet

The person who played the greatest role in shaping Jesse's ideas as a boy was his grandmother, "Aunt Tibby." "She made great sacrifices for my mother and me in our early years," he said.

Although she was unable to read and write, Aunt Tibby gave

young Jesse lessons one might not find between the pages of a book. She taught him to take pride in himself and to treat other people fairly. Her most important instruction to him was to aim high and be the best that he could be in life.

Every day her voice sang out with the rich black folk sayings that were passed from one generation to the next. Jesse always remembered them. Aunt Tibby made Jesse promise her that he would be somebody. She was fond of expressions like "Cleanliness is next to godliness." And she meant cleanliness in both appearance and character. "Ain't no such word as *can't. Can't* got drowned in the soda bottle" was something Aunt Tibby might say; so was "Nothing is impossible for those who love the Lord."

Aunt Tibby was a very religious woman. Speaking of her religious faith, Jesse Jackson told an audience before her death: "My grandmother doesn't have any education. She can't read or write, but she's never lost. She knows the worth of prayer. To the world she has no name, and she has no face, but she feels that she has importance because there's a God she communicates with who is eternal. And so she knows that every hardship is temporary. She used to tell me, 'Son, just hold on; there's joy in the morning.'"

Her special words of wisdom were what helped Jesse through his difficult moments as a boy. His grandmother's love and strength helped him sort through the mixed feelings that continued to come up from time to time about his natural father.

Aunt Tibby taught him that there was a reward for hard work and that he should not waste time. She said, "An idle mind is the devil's workshop." This saying meant that when a person was not busy doing something worthwhile, it was easy to get into trouble. And Jesse found this to be true.

Jesse was nicknamed Bo Diddley by family and friends, after a famous rock-and-roll singer. Bo Diddley recorded a song that was popular among black teens during the 1950s. It had a distinctive beat, and was later recorded by many other bands. The Bo Diddley in this song was a character who was always on the move—a real "earth-shaker," as they said in the 1950s. Perhaps this is why Jesse was given the nickname.

Young Bo Diddley Jesse Jackson sometimes got in the same kind of mischief as the other neighborhood boys. From time to time as a teenager, he was able to slip away from the watchful eye of his parents and grandmother. He would sneak to the pool-room for a game with older boys. He learned to play cards for money, which was thought of as a sin by religious families like his. Many of the boyhood friends who Jesse "hung out" with shooting pool and playing cards are in jail today, he said. Some became alcoholics and drug addicts. But Jesse never got carried away. Hanging out was fun for him once in a while. He remembered the things his grandmother said. He knew that he could not carry out her wish of being somebody if he spent too much time just playing around.

Jesse's character was also made stronger by the fact that his family went to church. He and his brother Charles attended Sunday school at the Longbranch Baptist Church, where his mother and stepfather sang in the choir. The church offered African-American children the opportunity to learn public speaking at an early age. They were always encouraged to come forward and make speeches in front of the congregation. By the age of four, Jesse was acting in church plays. His memory was good, and he was not afraid to face an audience. Old people smiled warmly as he made speeches. They would sit shaking their heads and saying how grand he sounded. The proudest person was Aunt Tibby. Her dreams for her daughter had not come true. But they might come true for her grandson.

The confidence that young Jesse developed at home carried over to his school life. He was a good student in elementary school. Jesse was not the perfect schoolboy, however. There are reports of his being a "cutup" and cracking jokes in class at times. But this was not his standard behavior. He knew there was too big a price to pay for "cuttin' up."

Throughout the South, many black teachers saw nothing

wrong with whipping a student from time to time. Parents usually went along with the teacher. They often gave the child a second paddling when they learned that he or she had not been behaving.

Jesse had to be whacked a time or two—but not that often. There were just too many people to answer to for any misconduct. There was the teacher, the parents, the preacher—a whole team who got in the act! These grown-ups generally knew one another, and they reported back and forth. Jesse couldn't get away with a bad deed at school even if he tried! If his teacher didn't see his mother on the way home, the two might meet on Saturday in the beauty shop or in the grocery store. Or they might run into each other in church on Sunday morning. And many teachers thought nothing of stopping by students' houses to discuss the children's schoolwork and activities. There was no escaping. Jesse said that this close-knit circle kept him and his peers out of trouble at school.

Responding to a question about his school years, Jesse Jackson said, "My mother took me to school that first day and said to Miss Georgeann Robinson, 'This is my boy. I want you to help him develop. He gets out of hand every now and then; therefore you might have to chastise him. If you do, send a note home, and he'd better bring it. If I don't see you at the PTA, because I work at night, I'll see you at church on Sunday." Jesse's mother told the school principal the same thing.

A sixth-grade teacher, Mrs. Sara Shelton, knew Jesse at age 12. He was tall and handsome and had a sparkling personality, she remembered. Mrs. Shelton recalled that Jesse was not too serious about his studies then. This was the time when Jesse first began hanging out. Mrs. Shelton said that, like many 12-year-old boys, Jesse started to look upon school as a place to have fun. "I thought nothing of putting him in his place with a smack of the ruler," she said. Afterward, Mrs. Shelton would report to his mother about his behavior.

"I used to tell him that the only chance he had to be somebody was to learn while it was easy—while he was young and had nothing else to do but learn," Mrs. Shelton recalled.

A final warning from her to Jesse was that it was his own responsibility to make something of himself. If he failed, he had no one to blame but himself. The things that Sara Shelton said were not much different from what Aunt Tibby had told Jesse. But the message came twice. Jesse thought deeply about what he'd been told. He knew that the advice was right. Time was precious. He would not be able to get the days of his youth back again.

So Jesse stopped wasting his time. He also stopped looking back. Everything had not been perfect in his past. But this was true for many people. The past could not be changed. What mattered was the future. This was where he decided to put his energies.

In no time Jesse became a student leader. He also became a good organizer. In order to raise money for a science project, he once volunteered his mother's home for a Sunday afternoon tea. Teas were popular events for boys and girls at this time. It gave them an opportunity to get together socially. Sometimes a person would recite a poem. Another person might sing a song. Punch, sandwiches, and other little snacks were served at a small price.

Fortunately, Jesse's mother went along with his big idea. The tea turned out to be the first of many successful events organized by Jesse Louis Jackson.

Later that year, Jesse became a member of the reading club at the County Library for Colored People. Public libraries in the South were open only to whites at this time. Black children had to use county libraries, small, one-room structures with few books. In Greenville, the county library was set up in the town's community center. Books were supplied by the white library, and sometimes people donated them. Like the used books in the classroom that were passed on from the white schools, the library books were not always in the best shape. Sometimes the young black readers would discover missing pages just when they were deep into a good story! Jesse had a huge appetite for new information. He even studied the dictionary for new words. As a result, he became well informed on many subjects and enjoyed expressing himself.

But Jesse was not all books. He knew how to laugh and keep a good joke going. People enjoyed his "jiving and teasing." Walking to school, he and his friends would pass white students on their way to the all-white school. Jesse and the other black children had to walk six miles to get to school. His jokes helped make the walk seem shorter.

Noah, Jr., his half brother, returned to Greenville by the time the boys reached high school. The two boys grew closer. Noah recalls Jesse being a king of comedy. It pleased Noah to see how well Jesse held the attention of a crowd at the table in the school lunchroom. All the boys and girls liked him.

By ninth grade, Jesse was excelling in his studies. He had become quite a leader in school. He was elected president of his class and president of the Honor Society. Students had to maintain an 80 or above average grade to be in the Honor Society. Being elected president of this group was a very high honor. All of the teachers in the school paid special attention to the president of the Honor Society. Jesse enjoyed the good feeling that came with this special role.

In school, he was learning how to be the best at all the activities in which he took part. From president of the Honor Society to presidential candidate—for him it was just a matter of time.

SOCIAL PROTEST

66 We shall overcome.
We shall overcome.
We shall overcome, someday.
For deep in our hearts
we do believe
that we shall overcome
someday. 99

**AFRICAN-AMERICAN FREEDOM
SONG**

Throughout his childhood, Jesse worked in a variety of jobs. As a very young boy, he worked at a shoe-shine stand, and he helped a family friend chop and sell fire-wood. Jesse was the first black boy to be a salesperson in the concession stands at white football games. As a teenager, he worked for white golf players, carrying their golf clubs. A favorite job was working as a ticket collector for the Liberty Movie Theatre in Greenville. Everyone wanted to be Jesse's friend while he worked at the movies because sometimes he let people sneak in for free.

It was while working at Claussen's Bakery that Jesse took a stand against racism. Along with a friend, Owen Perkins, Jesse cleaned the bakery machines at Claussen's on weekends. The two boys decided that they would protest the bad conditions of their workplace. There were Whites Only rest rooms and drinking fountains at the bakery. They tried to organize the other black employees to hold a protest, but they were not successful. The workers were too afraid of losing their jobs.

Jesse had gotten the idea to protest from the Reverend James Hall, a local, young black preacher. The Reverend James Hall was a member of the National Association for the Advancement of Colored People, or the NAACP. The NAACP was working for school integration and other social issues that affected blacks.

Hall had led a protest over an incident that involved Jackie Robinson, the first black man ever to become a major league baseball player in the United States. Jackie Robinson was turned away from a Greenville restaurant. Hall felt that it was an insult for a hero such as Jackie Robinson to be treated so badly. So he organized a protest march against the restaurant.

The courage of the Reverend James Hall, someone right there in Greenville, inspired Jesse to speak up. Jesse knew that he and his coworkers at Claussen's Bakery were not famous like the great Jackie Robinson. But he knew that they certainly had every right to be treated with respect and dignity. Although the protest was not successful, Jesse felt good about his effort. He knew that he was right. This was his first lesson in what Hall called "social action."

Sermons that Jesse Jackson heard from the Reverend James Hall would stay with him for years. Today, remembering what he heard as a boy helps Jesse with his own speeches. Speaking of Hall in one of his talks, Jesse recalled: "When I was a child in Greenville, South Carolina, the Reverend James Hall used to preach a sermon every so often with a quote saying, 'If I be lifted up, I'll draw all men unto me.' When I was a child I didn't

Thurgood Marshall, NAACP officer, later became the first African-American Supreme Court justice.

quite understand what he meant. But I understand better now. If you raise up truth, it's magnetic. It has a way of drawing people."

Although Jesse was too young to know all the details, the NAACP was doing many things to change conditions for young African Americans like him. In 1954, when Jesse was 13, the NAACP won a major fight against school segregation. The case was called *Brown* v. *the Board of Education of Topeka* (Kansas). It was led by NAACP lawyers. Among the lawyers was Thurgood Marshall, who later became the first black to be named to be a justice on the Supreme Court of the United States.

Up until this time, segregation in schools was legal. It had been made legal by an 1896 Supreme Court decision called *Plessy* v. *Ferguson*. This decision said that segregation, or separation, of the races was all right if each group was given equal facilities. One problem with this rule was that blacks were not given equal facilities. The white schools, libraries, public rest rooms, and movie theaters were always better. The NAACP had worked for years to overturn the rule. The *Brown* case said that separate schools were not equal—and, therefore, no longer legal. That meant that other laws keeping blacks separate would be illegal, too.

When he was 14, Jesse learned of another major social protest. It was the Montgomery Bus Boycott of 1955. Blacks of Montgomery, Alabama, refused to ride the city buses for an entire year. They were protesting segregation and unfair treatment.

The bus rules in Montgomery were the same rules that existed throughout the South. Blacks had to drop their money in the box at the front of the bus. Then they had to walk around to the back door to get into the bus. Drivers often drove away before they could even get inside. If they made it inside the bus, blacks had to take seats in back. When all of the seats up front—where whites sat—became filled, blacks had to give up their seats to the whites.

On December 1, 1955, a black seamstress, Rosa Parks, had had enough. She said no when a bus driver demanded that she give up her seat to a white person. Her feet were tired, and she didn't want to stand the whole way home. Rosa Parks, who happened to be an active member of the NAACP, was arrested. When the NAACP leaders learned what had happened, they decided to help the local blacks protest. The black people of Montgomery banded together and refused to ride the buses.

Rosa Parks enters the courthouse in Montgomery, Alabama, to face charges in the 1955 bus boycott.

For 381 days the black citizens staged a boycott against the city buses. Finally, they returned to the buses—but not before they changed the laws so that they would be treated equally. They also succeeded in getting blacks hired as bus drivers. This was not an easy victory. Homes of members of the Montgomery Improvement Association, the group of local black leaders who organized the boycott, were bombed. Some blacks were beaten. Others lost their jobs. Only through strong organization, good leadership, and religious faith were they able to win.

Buses remain empty in Montgomery as protesters continue their boycott.

During the bus boycott, special leadership came from Dr. Martin Luther King, Jr. One day he would become Jesse Jackson's hero. Born on January 15, 1929, in Atlanta, Georgia, King was the son of a Baptist minister. He and his wife, Coretta Scott, moved to Montgomery in 1954, where King became the minister of the Dexter Avenue Baptist Church. King was chosen by the Montgomery Improvement Association to give leadership to the protest.

While in school, King had read the works of Henry David Thoreau. Thoreau was an American who lived during the 1800s. He had written about the citizens protesting against unjust laws. King also studied the life of Mohandas Karamchand Gandhi. Gandhi helped to free India from the rule of the British. He used social protest to bring about change. King combined everything he learned with his religious training. He asked blacks to be nonviolent. As they demonstrated against racial segregation, the people sang songs of freedom, such as "We Shall Overcome":

> We shall overcome.
> We shall overcome.
> We shall overcome, someday.
> For deep in our hearts
> We do believe
> That we shall overcome someday.

This haunting hymn was to become a theme song for the civil rights movement as it spread across America. This song and the struggle that took place in Montgomery were taught in Jesse's high school and in black schools across the South. A new pride was growing among young people as they heard of the progress of Dr. King and his followers. They saw hope for themselves in the Montgomery victory.

HIGH SCHOOL YEARS AND BEYOND

66 *Don't let them see you cry.* **99**

A white reporter talking
to Elizabeth Eckford, one
of the Little Rock Nine

esse was inspired by black leaders such as Martin Luther King, Jr. Encouraged by his parents and teachers, Jesse continued to study hard throughout high school. One teacher, Xanthene Norris, said that Jesse was very vocal. He spoke out often in class. Mrs. Norris, also taught Jesse's half brother Noah. She said that the two brothers were opposites in terms of how they expressed themselves. She practically had to

pull words out of Noah. Jesse, on the other hand, was always talking, she said.

Though he was jealous of Noah when he was younger, Jesse no longer felt that way during their high school years. Not only was Jesse gifted with words, but he was also a talented athlete. He continued to be a leader in school, coming out on top at almost everything. As his popularity grew, jealous students began to complain to teachers. They wanted to know why he was always the leader of everything. Little did they know that Jesse had only just begun.

Jesse was an all-around athlete. He received letters (special high school awards) in baseball, football, and basketball.

Charles Jackson had turned down a career in baseball at the time he married Jesse's mother. Mr. Jackson took special interest in Jesse and his brother Charles's school sports. He attended their school games and offered pointers on how they could improve their play.

Jesse's high school football coach, J. D. Mathis, worked with him from age 13 to 17. Coach Mathis said that Jesse was bigger and stronger than most of the linemen. "He was swift and clean in his play," said the coach, "an all-American type." Coach Mathis made sure his boys were more than just good athletes. He insisted that his players work on improving their minds along with improving their game.

Coach Mathis did not have to worry about Jesse. When the team was playing a game out of town, Jesse would stop by his classes to pick up his homework. It would have been easy for him to avoid doing this. Many of the black high school games across the South were played on school nights. Black schools usually shared their football stadiums with the white schools. The white schools always got first choice of which nights they wanted to use the stadiums. Naturally, the whites picked the weekends, and so the black students played during the week. Some boys on the team thought nothing of using this as an excuse for not doing their homework. But not Jesse. He did his schoolwork, and he played a great game, too.

There was discrimination in the local news coverage of the football games, as well. Jesse once scored three touchdowns in a game. His school won with a winning score of 20 to 6. The all-white high school won its game 7 to 6. The white school's star quarterback, Dickie Dietz, had kicked the extra point. There was a big headline spread across the paper the next day reading, "Dietz Kicks Extra Point, Greenville Wins." The story about Jesse was on the bottom of the page stating, "Jackson Makes Three Touchdowns, Sterling Wins."

There was nothing that Jesse or his black schoolmates could do about the unfair treatment. Their teachers and parents felt equally helpless. But they were not without hope. Their hope rested with the fact that the NAACP had been victorious with the *Brown* case.

Success in the *Brown* case was the result of one young person's special courage. Her name was Barbara Johns. Johns was a 16-year-old black student who attended school in Virginia. On April 23, 1951, she called a meeting of her fellow students. She spoke harshly against the tar-paper shacks that the county had built to serve as schools for black children. The schools were overcrowded. Students had to wear their coats inside throughout the winter. Teachers had to gather wood and start fires early in the morning. Barbara said that the students should call a strike. They should stay away from school until some improvements were made. She said that even if the changes didn't come in time to help them, they could help younger black children. The NAACP said they would help the students in their protest. But instead of demanding better schools for blacks, they decided to sue for integrated schools. A few members of the black community questioned whether this was the right time to act. A young black preacher rose in a mass meeting and shouted, "Anybody who would not back these children after they stepped out on a limb is not a man." And that ended the discussion.

The NAACP added Barbara Johns's statements to other lawsuits against school segregation. Her ideas, the *Brown* suit, and other complaints that the NAACP had received were all combined. Together, they became the historic *Brown* decision, which was won on May 24, 1954.

Although this Court ruling declared that school segregation was illegal, southern schools remained segregated. It appeared that few whites were taking the law seriously.

Southern towns went right on running their schools however they pleased. Some made excuses, saying the law was not clear enough. Others took small steps, such as allowing one or two black students to attend white schools. But most southern towns kept totally separate black and white schools. Jesse's school was segregated.

Many black students were relieved that no attempt at integration had been made in their hometown. This was especially true after a major crisis took place. The crisis occurred as black and white students integrated at Central High School in Little Rock, Arkansas. The year was 1957. Jesse Jackson was 16 years old.

The tense scene in Arkansas brought fear to blacks, young and old. One person who showed great courage during the school integration in Arkansas was a 15-year-old named Elizabeth Eckford. She was one of "the Little Rock Nine," as the black students who wanted to go to the white high school were called. On the first day of school, all of the Little Rock Nine were supposed to meet at the home of Daisy Bates, the president of the local NAACP. Then they were to travel to school together in a group. Unfortunately, Elizabeth Eckford had no phone, and, somehow, the message did not reach her. She set out for school alone. Elizabeth soon found herself walking alone through a crowd of mean, angry whites, who were shouting and throwing rocks at her.

"Lynch her! Lynch her!" the crowd shouted as she tried to enter the school. Some threw garbage at her; others shouted curses and spit at her. The guards who were supposed to protect the Little Rock Nine offered no help.

"No nigger...is going to get in our school!" someone from the mob screamed. "Get out of here!"

A white reporter walked up to Elizabeth and said, "Don't let them see you cry." As the crowd grew uglier, one brave white woman came to the young girl's rescue. Taking Elizabeth by the arm, she led her away. The two then took a bus back to Elizabeth's home. At first Elizabeth's father said that he was not going to let her return to Central High. But after she pleaded with him to let her try again, she bravely set out again the next day. Other black parents were worried about the danger their

Gloria Ray | Terrance Roberts | Melba Patillo

Elizabeth Eckford | Ernest Green | MinniJean Brown

Jefferson Thomas | Carlotta Walls | Thelma Mothershed

THE LITTLE ROCK NINE

Federal troops were sent to Central High School to protect the Little Rock Nine, pictured here.

children faced. The children continued in spite of their fears.

Central High was eventually integrated. But not without the help of the president of the United States, who had to send in military troops. Even with the troops there, the black students had to endure endless insults and abuse every day. One girl could not stand the pressure and was sent north by her parents.

The integration of Central High was followed by racist cries all across the South. Segregationists vowed that blacks would never attend white schools in their towns! Jesse and his friends heard that change might come to Greenville. But there was no sign of it when he graduated from all-black Sterling High School in 1959.

When Jesse finished high school, he was offered a job playing baseball for the New York Giants. The Chicago White Sox offered him a better deal—$6,000 to play for their team. Jesse thought that this was a good offer. Then he learned that the same team had offered Dickie Dietz, the white high school star, much more. This made him so mad that he decided not to play professional baseball at all! Instead, he accepted a scholarship to play football for the University of Illinois.

Jesse had been a star quarterback in Greenville. So naturally he went to the university expecting to play this position there. In football, the quarterback is looked upon as the leader of the team. What Jesse discovered was that the quarterback position was not given to blacks at integrated colleges. Black players were expected to be in the backup positions in the game.

Other parts of college life disappointed Jesse, too. In the South, he'd been a member of a special community. People had known his name everywhere he went. He'd been in the spotlight back home. There had been places where he and his friends could get together in Greenville. But up North, Jesse felt lost. White fraternities and sororities had special houses where they held parties. But the college clubs for black students were too poor to own buildings. They had no rich parents or sponsors who had left money for them to buy buildings.

While the white students enjoyed parties in their special houses, the blacks had to go to the Veterans of Foreign Wars Lodge and other such clubs for their dances. Jesse recalls one night when Lionel Hampton, a famous black musician, came to the school. "The whites were jumping to Lionel Hampton in the gym," he says, "and we weren't even invited!"

Jesse discovered that in spite of the stories he had heard about things being different up North, there was discrimination there, too. "Up South!" was how some southern blacks who had traveled north described it.

One year at the University of Illinois was enough to convince Jesse that he wanted to return to the South to study. His choice was North Carolina Agricultural and Technical State University in Greensboro. There was a special reason that Jesse decided on North Carolina A & T. Students from that college had staged the first sit-in.

THE YOUNG ONES STEP IN

66 Hold your head high, stick your chest out. You can make it. It gets dark sometimes but the morning comes. Don't you surrender. Suffering breeds character. Character breeds faith. So in the end faith will not disappoint. 99

JESSE JACKSON

The following is a description of a sit-in:

Imagine that you are a teenager thirty years ago sitting on a stool at a lunch counter somewhere in the South. If you were a white and you ordered a sandwich, you could just sit there and calmly eat it. If you were a black, however, you would have broken the law if you had even sat down. Blacks were not allowed to sit at lunch counters and eat. If you had sat down as a way of protest against these unjust laws, you might have had

These young men were arrested in Little Rock for sitting-in at a lunch counter.

catsup poured all over your head. You might have even been beaten up and hauled off to jail—just for trying to order lunch.

The first of these student sit-ins took place in 1960. Four students from North Carolina A & T—Izell Blair, Franklin McCain, Joseph McNeil, and David Richmond—tried to integrate the local Woolworth's luncheonette. They took seats at the counter and tried to order coffee. They were refused and told to move on. Whites gathered around the students. They cursed and shoved them. The group remained until the store closed. During the next few days, more young people came and sat at the counter. Soon, other groups of black students across the South were doing the same thing. Many white students joined them. This was the beginning of the 1960s sit-in movement by college students. Jesse wanted to be involved in it.

As the sit-ins spread, the students decided to organize themselves. Ella Baker was one of the black adult leaders who helped them. Baker was executive director of the Southern Christian Leadership Conference, or the SCLC. This was an organization that Dr. Martin Luther King, Jr., and other southern African-American clergymen had organized when the Montgomery boycotts ended. The SCLC was formed to continue work for equal rights in the South.

Both the SCLC and the NAACP wanted the students to become a special part of their organizations. Instead, the students called themselves "grassroots people." They used this term to describe ordinary people, the ones from the community, without any special labels attached to them.

Ella Baker urged the young people to form their own group—an organization that wouldn't take orders from one leader. She encouraged them to form a group in which the members would make decisions together. The students agreed with Baker. The leaders of the different student sit-ins came together in Raleigh, North Carolina, in 1960. Among the young people were white students. They formed the Student Nonviolent Coordinating Committee, or SNCC. Dr. King spoke at this gathering.

Afterward, the students issued a paper that outlined their purpose. The influence of King was obvious, for they spoke of nonviolence, love, and peace throughout the statement.

Along with the teachings of nonviolence that King gave the SNCC student members, they received training from the Reverend James Lawson. He was studying at Vanderbilt University in Tennessee. There, he had led workshops on nonviolence. Lawson had also served as a missionary in India. So, like King, he knew a lot about passive resistance through the teachings of Gandhi. Thus the students were well prepared for how they were to conduct themselves when the demonstrations grew.

Once he was back in the South, Jesse immediately became involved in the student sit-ins. At A & T, he was elected president of the student body and an officer of the Omega Psi Phi fraternity. The quarterback position he had hoped for in Illinois was his at A & T. In spite of all the extra activities, Jesse continued to do well in his studies and was as popular as ever with girls. His reading included books by the great African-

American theologian Howard Thurman and the African-American scholar W. E. B. Du Bois.

Eventually, Jesse's ability to speak well helped him become a leader in the sit-in movements. When CORE, the Congress of Racial Equality, came to Greensboro to stage a major demonstration, Jesse was called upon to organize the students. CORE was a civil rights organization that had been in existence since the 1940s. When the SNCC students needed more support for their movement, they turned to CORE. Many of the students were suspended from some of the black colleges for their activities. The college officials who relied on state money for their salaries, as well as to operate their schools, began to put pressure on students. These college officials asked students at their schools to slow down with the sit-ins, and in some instances, to stop their activity completely. The students had hoped that the SCLC would help them more. When this did not happen, they turned to CORE.

The leaders of CORE were glad that the students came to them. The students could help test a new government order. In 1960, the federal Interstate Commerce Commission ordered that all businesses, restaurants, and rest rooms on interstate highways be integrated. In 1961, CORE tested that order with a demonstration that was to capture national attention called the Freedom Rides. The Freedom Riders were integrated groups of people who boarded buses and traveled through the South. Many young people were anxious to see the civil rights movement advance, so they joined the Freedom Rides.

The young Freedom Riders took great risks as their buses made stops across the country. Some of them were badly beaten as they tried to sit in white–only waiting rooms or at white lunch counters. White southerners bombed the first Freedom Ride bus. At one point, bus drivers began to refuse to drive the Freedom Riders out of fear for their own lives. CORE was forced to call upon President John F. Kennedy to protect the Freedom Riders.

President Kennedy's brother Robert was head of the Justice Department. He gave the kind of help that was needed. He sent helicopters to hover over the buses. Cars also traveled the routes of the Freedom Riders. This was a lot of protection. But it was not enough. Southern racists continued to attack the Freedom Riders at every point they could.

One of the many whites who traveled south was Jim Zwerg. He had traveled all the way from Wisconsin to take part. Zwerg was beaten so badly in Alabama that he had to be hospitalized. The news media from across the country were now covering the events. People were shocked to see the horror of what was happening. Reporters interviewed Jim Zwerg at his bedside. Zwerg declared that segregation must end. He vowed that the

Freedom Rides would continue. "We're dedicated to this," he said. "We will take hitting. We'll take beatings. We're willing to accept death...but we are going to keep coming until we can ride anywhere in the South as Americans, without anyone making comments."

One of President Kennedy's representatives was attacked in Birmingham. After that, the president sent in even more government people. Special security forces surrounded the hospital. Additional guards traveled along with the Freedom Riders as they continued their journey.

Jesse's association with CORE made it possible for him to meet important civil rights figures of the day. He had yet to meet Dr. King, but he was getting closer to that important moment in his life.

Jesse got more and more involved with other students working in the movement. As he did so, he became attracted to a young woman who shared his interests. Her name was Jacqueline Lavinia Brown. Jacqueline was one year behind Jesse in college. He was impressed by her commitment to the struggle, her personality, and her good looks. Jacqueline was equally impressed with Jesse and was pleased to date someone who had the same values. Jacqueline learned that, in addition to all his special qualities, Jesse also attended church. The two began to attend together. They fell in love and were married in the home of Jesse's parents in Greenville.

In 1963, Jesse took part in a sit-in and was arrested for demonstrating. He was released from jail when their first child was born. It was a girl whom they named Santita. Because Jacqueline and Jesse both believed so strongly in the cause of civil rights, they worked hand in hand. As the baby grew, they took her along with them to civil rights gatherings.

The Jacksons were a struggling young couple with little money. Jacqueline said that it was a time when people across the country were standing together. She said that even the doctor who delivered Santita did not charge them any money. Many

PROTEST DEMONSTRATIONS IN THE SOUTH

Legend:
- Bus Boycott
- Demonstrations
- Freedom Ride Stop
- March
- Student Sit-ins
- School Integration
- ★ State Capital

ATLANTIC OCEAN

GULF OF MEXICO

Washington, D.C.

Richmond ★
VIRGINIA

Raleigh ★
Greensboro •
NORTH CAROLINA

Columbia ★
SOUTH CAROLINA

St. Augustine

FLORIDA

Frankfort ★
KENTUCKY

Knoxville ★
Nashville •
TENNESSEE

Atlanta ★
GEORGIA
Albany •

Tallahassee ★

Anniston •
Birmingham •
Tuscaloosa •
Selma • Montgomery ★
ALABAMA

Memphis •

Oxford •
Meridian •
Jackson •
MISSISSIPPI

Mobile •

Little Rock ★
ARKANSAS

Baton Rouge ★
New Orleans •
LOUISIANA

N
W—E
S

0   100   200

people, both black and white, were eager to see a new day in America. However they could, with time or money, they were all trying to help toward that day.

Jesse saw the very important role that not only King but also other ministers were playing in the movement. Churches were a center of black activity in the South, and the people respected the pastors who led them.

Jesse was pleased to see the growing role that young people were having in the movement. Hundreds of youths were being arrested across the country as they demonstrated for desegregation. One such place was Albany, Georgia, where from 1961 until 1965, blacks protested. Jesse followed events there as Martin Luther King, Jr., took part in demonstrations in this troubled town. But even the presence of King was not enough to prevent the city officials from bending the laws to their advantage.

Birmingham, Alabama, was targeted as the next city in which to hold major demonstrations. African Americans across the South knew that Birmingham was one of the most racist towns in the nation. Because of this, it surprised people that King planned to let children march. One answer that King gave was that adults who demonstrated could lose their jobs. But young people did not face that risk. Even so, many did not think this was a wise decision. They felt that children, especially very young ones, should not be placed at risk.

But the young people begged to march. It was their future that was at stake. Black children were tired of getting ragged, used books from white schools. They were tired of using scratched, old desks discarded from the white schools. White schools got new things—new things that the tax dollars of black mothers and fathers helped pay for. It was better that the children demonstrated then for their freedom. If not, their younger sisters and brothers, and maybe even their own children, would have had to live as second-class citizens. So it was "Freedom now!" they shouted as they prepared to demonstrate.

Firemen turn their hoses on a crowd during the Birmingham protests against segregation.

The children had no idea what they were headed for, however. Eugene "Bull" Connor, the public safety commissioner, set attack dogs and fire hoses on the youthful demonstrators. At night on television, every day in the newspapers, Jesse Jackson and millions of Americans watched the horror of Birmingham. There were terrible scenes of fierce police dogs snarling with their fangs bared. Many young people were bitten and had their clothes torn. The protesters continued to march peacefully and chant, "Freedom now!" Then the order was given to turn the fire hoses on the children. A fire hose at close range has so much power that it can lift a person up and slam him or her against a building. Many young people were hurt by the fire hoses.

Americans watched young people—even children—being beaten and abused on Freedom Rides in Birmingham and in student sit-ins. These brutal scenes touched the conscience of the nation. As a result, more people, black and white, decided to join the civil rights movement.

ACCEPTING THE CALL

> **❝** *I have a dream that my four little children will one day live in a nation where they will not be judged by the color of their skin, but the content of their character.* **❞**
>
> MARTIN LUTHER KING, JR.

After graduating from college in 1963, Jesse Jackson thought more and more about becoming a minister. He also thought about studying law. Jackson knew how important lawyers could be to the movement. But then he still remembered the important role of the ministers.

Before he graduated, Jesse Jackson called on Dr. Samuel Proctor, the campus minister and president of his college. He wanted to discuss the possibility of his becoming a preacher. In certain Christian churches, there is what is known as a "call" to preach. Many preachers tell stories of when they were called. For them it is a kind of special signal that comes to them, telling them that they were born to preach.

One morning when Jackson was in college, he woke up and told his roommate that he had had an odd dream.

Jesse thought that the dream was the call to preach. "He was shaking. I never saw him so serious," said his roommate.

When Jesse was 14, he had told his father, Noah Robinson, about another dream. In this dream he led an army across water as Moses had done in the Bible story. His father reminded Jesse that his grandfather had been a fine preacher and that he, too, could be one someday.

Proctor advised Jesse to take the call to preach seriously. Jesse listened, but did not make a decision right away. Instead, he worked for the governor of North Carolina, Terry Sanford, for a short while. The job was to organize clubs for young Democrats. Jesse found the political work meaningful, but he had not forgotten Proctor's words. He also wanted to be more involved in the movement. He wanted to do the kind of work he had done while in college. Jesse could not stop thinking about what had happened to the young people in the struggle at Birmingham. He recalled the children being hosed down and attacked by dogs.

During the Birmingham riots, King had been jailed. While in jail, he wrote a long statement. It was an answer for whites who questioned the timing of the demonstrations in Birmingham. The whites had been saying things like, "Be patient. Wait a little longer and things will work out. Stop demonstrating." In this statement, King told them why African Americans could wait no longer. The answer he gave had deep spiritual meaning for Jesse. Dr. King said to the white critics:

> When you have seen vicious mobs lynch your mothers and
> fathers at will and drown your sisters and brothers at
> whim; when you have seen hate-filled policemen curse,

kick, brutalize and even kill your black brothers and sisters . . . when you see the vast majority of your twenty million Negro brothers smothering in an air-tight cage of poverty in the midst of a [rich] society, when you suddenly find your tongue twisted and your speech stammering as you seek to explain to your six-year-old daughter why she can't go to the public amusement park that has just been advertised on television, and see tears welling up in her little eyes when she is told that Funtown is closed to colored children . . . when you take a cross-country drive and find it necessary to sleep night after night in the uncomfortable corners of your automobile because no motel will accept you; when you are humiliated day in and day out by nagging signs reading "white" and "colored"; when you are forever fighting a degenerating sense of "nobodiness"; and then you will understand why it is difficult to wait.

The powerful words of Dr. Martin Luther King, Jr., and all that he stood for drew Jackson closer to the ministry.

In August 1963, when Jackson was 22 years old, King captured the full attention of an audience of more than 1 million people. This was at the famous March on Washington, where he gave his unforgettable "I Have a Dream" speech. People of all races from across the country traveled to Washington, D.C., that day. The purpose was to demand equal opportunity for blacks seeking better jobs and housing and to urge members of the government to vote for civil rights laws.

The march had been the idea of A. Philip Randolph. Randolph was so respected that he was called "Father" or the "Saint" by others in the movement. He had founded the Brotherhood of Sleeping Car Porters in 1925. The BSCP, as it was called, was an organization of African Americans who worked on the nation's trains as servants, cooking and cleaning. Many of the members of the BSCP were college-educated men. But because of racism, they were forced to take this kind of low-level job.

A. Philip Randolph led the fight for equality in the work-place for African Americans.

Better jobs were not open to them. This was the sort of thing that Randolph wanted to see end. He had organized to protect the rights of the train porters in their particular jobs. He had been working for civil rights for African Americans in other areas, too. The March on Washington, D.C., was very important to him.

Among the many black groups coming together for the March on Washington, there was a mixture of ideas. Some of the young blacks were more militant and less patient than the older civil rights workers. One of these was Malcolm X.

Malcolm X was a black Muslim leader who taught methods of struggle other than nonviolence. Malcolm X did not teach violence, but he was in favor of blacks using force if they were attacked. Malcolm X and Martin Luther King, Jr., were never enemies, as some people claim, but they did view the struggle differently. Malcolm X's life, like that of so many leaders who dared to speak out against racism, ended in tragedy. He was assassinated as he spoke before a crowd in New York in 1965. He left behind a pregnant wife and four children.

The influence that Malcolm X had on young people caused King to think more about his ideas. A lot of what Malcolm X said made sense. He believed you should try to reason with a person who is trying to harm you. But if reasoning does not work, you have no choice but to try something else. Unfortunately, this "something else" could mean violence. But violence as a first choice was not Malcolm X's way.

At the time of the March on Washington, many of the young people were very angry. They were angry about all the violence that had taken place. Between 1957 and 1963, 17 black churches had been bombed in Birmingham, Alabama, alone. More homes than that were destroyed. People were beaten and killed. Since the murder of Emmett Till in Mississippi, there had been other murders.

Malcolm X (middle), a leader of northern blacks, shown with Rep. Adam Clayton Powell, Jr. (left).

Two deaths in particular captured the headlines. These were the murders of Medgar Evers, who was field director for the NAACP, and Herbert Lee, a young SNCC worker. Both men were shot by white racists for their role in the movement. But no one stood trial for their murders. Their widows were among the women given special recognition at the March on Washington. The presence of these women was a sad reminder to the young people of the horrors that African-American people had endured.

They were reminded also by seeing Fannie Lou Hamer there, a sharecropper from Mississippi. Hamer had been severely beaten for her involvement in the struggle. She had been arrested in Winona, Mississippi, along with some other Freedom Riders. Hamer was dragged into an empty cell and thrown face down on a cot. The sheriff ordered a young black prisoner to beat her with a blackjack. A second prisoner was ordered to sit on her legs. Hamer tried to protect her head with her hands. Her hands were beaten severely. Her back was beaten until it was swollen, and her body became as hard as stone. Even so, Hamer said that she forgave the young black man who had beaten her, for she knew that he had had no choice.

Many older members of the movement were able to forgive this way. The younger members were less patient, however. The representative for the young SNCC workers at the march was John Lewis, who had been in the sit-ins and the Freedom Rides. Lewis wrote a speech with other SNCC workers. One of these workers was young Stokely Carmichael. Carmichael leaned more toward the teachings of Malcolm X than those of King. Lewis and the others wanted the crowd to hear a radical speech, one that expressed how angry he and other young people were about the state of black people in the country. Lewis wanted the government to be warned that they were not going to sit still and quietly protest.

Lewis's speech was read in advance by Bayard Rustin, one of the planners of the march. The speech disturbed Rustin and some of the older organizers. They felt that the tone was too fiery. They worried that it might hurt the efforts of A. Philip Randolph and the older civil rights veterans. Rustin did not want to risk having the "Young Turks," as they were called, turn the march into a less than peaceful demonstration. So he pleaded with them to tone down their message.

Out of respect for Randolph, John Lewis and the Young Turks decided to rewrite the speech. Their decision was a good one for everyone involved. It was important that there be unity at this historic gathering when all of America was watching. Although women were not invited to give major speches, many women, including Ella Baker and Fannie Lou Hamer, had played key roles in the movement. The women's names were read off in a special tribute, and Marian Anderson and Mahalia Jackson sang.

Dr. King's speech was the high point of the March on Washington. It captured the attention of not only Jesse Jackson but of all Americans as well. In ringing words, Martin Luther King, Jr., told of his dream for America. The best part of the speech came when Dr. King looked away from his notes and spoke from his heart. This was the style he used while preaching from the pulpit in church. His voice reaching higher tones toward the end of the speech, King said:

> I say to you today, my friends, so even though we face the difficulties of today and tomorrow, I still have a dream.... It is a dream deeply rooted in the American meaning of its creed, "We hold these truths to be self-evident, that all men are created equal." I have a dream that one day on the red hills of Georgia, sons of former slaves and sons of former slave owners will be able to sit down together at the table of brotherhood.... I have a dream that my four little children will one day live in a nation where they will not be judged by the color of their skin, but the content of their character.

Crowds at the 1963 March on Washington listen to Martin Luther King's "I Have a Dream" speech.

I have a dream today!

I have a dream that one day...little black boys and black girls will be able to join hands with little white boys and white girls as sisters and brothers.

I have a dream today!

I have a dream that one day...all God's children will be able to sing with new meaning, "My country 'tis of thee, sweet land of liberty, of thee I sing. Land where my fathers died, land of the pilgrim's pride, from every mountainside, let freedom ring." And if America is to be a great nation, this must come true. . . .

And when this happens and when we allow freedom to ring, when we let it ring from every village and every hamlet, from every state and every city, we will be able to speed up that day when all God's children, black men and white men, Jews and gentiles, Protestants and Catholics, will be able to join hands and sing in the words of the old Negro spiritual: "Free at last, Free at last. Thank God Almighty, we are free at last."

The March on Washington was a great success. For the first time in this country, people of all races and religions came together for a single cause. The march showed the beauty of such togetherness. It was a visible sign to the lawmakers of the country that indeed people really did want to see change in America.

But in spite of the March on Washington, Congress did not pass a civil rights law right away. All signs were leading in that direction, however. People sent letters to their representatives in Congress, asking them to vote for the bill. Many Americans knew that this was the right thing to do. But the hearts of some were still not changed.

Less than one month after the march, southern racists killed four young black girls in Birmingham, Alabama. A bomb had exploded at the Sixteenth Street Baptist Church. The girls were Denise McNair (age 11), Cynthia Wesley, Carol Robertson, and Addie Mae Collins (all age 14). This church was bombed because it was a meeting place for civil rights activists.

The murder of the young black girls shocked the nation. It was hard for the older leaders in the movement to contain the anger of the young militants now. Many wanted to take to the streets and fight.

THE STRUGGLE CONTINUES

> **" Without struggle there can be no progress. "**
>
> **FREDERICK DOUGLASS**

In 1965, Jesse Jackson finally decided to become a minister. He made up his mind that this would be the best way for him to serve his people. He enrolled in the Chicago Theological Seminary. Times were not easy then, but Jesse and Jacqueline were happy in the life they were building together. Jackson's early years of discipline paid off as he juggled the responsibilities of studies and work. Jacqueline helped by baby-sitting and working in the library.

The civil rights struggle was still important to the Jackson family. Jackson joined the Southern Christian Leadership Conference in Chicago and continued to watch what was taking place on the national scene.

By now, King had made great inroads in the South. Help for the movement came from many places. Concerned citizens who did not travel South to protest sent money and clothing. Many black sororities, fraternities, and social clubs outside of the South made the civil rights struggle their main order of business. Many young students graduating from college who might have taken good jobs or gone on to graduate school told their parents that, instead, they wanted to travel South to join the movement. Churches set up special programs in the South to help. Many teachers offered assistance.

At this time brave young white students, as well as blacks, were part of the civil rights movement. Two of them were killed for their efforts. Michael Schwerner and Andrew Goodman, along with a young black man, James Chaney, were murdered by white racists near Meridian, Mississippi, in June 1964. Three years later, an all-white jury found seven men guilty of murder. This was the first time that anyone had been convicted in the state of Mississippi for murdering civil rights workers.

As blacks continued to fight for the right to register to vote in the South, more lives were lost. Twenty-six-year-old Jimmy Lee Jackson became a victim in Marion, Alabama. A group of blacks trying to register to vote had been turned away in Selma, Alabama. A big confrontation took place between C. T. Vivian, the leader of this group, and Sheriff Jim Clark. Later, Vivian traveled to Marion to speak to citizens who lived there about what had happened. At the end of Vivian's speech, it started to get dark. The group held a nighttime march, something that was very dangerous. Before long, they were surrounded by angry whites, police, and state troopers. The whites turned out the city streetlights and attacked the blacks. Jimmy Lee Jackson's 82-year-old grandfather was bleeding, so Jackson rushed him into a nearby café. Troopers followed them and continued to beat the old man. Then one of the troopers hit Jackson's mother, and he defended her. Jackson was shot in the stomach and died seven days later. The SCLC called for a march from Selma to the state capitol in Montgomery. Dr. King announced that he would support the march from Selma to Montgomery.

The march began on March 7, 1965, but the demonstrators did not go far. An attack on the marchers was so vicious that the day became known as Bloody Sunday. Policemen on horseback rode into the crowd and threw tear gas at the group, which included many women and children. People were clubbed to the ground. Television crews who were filming the event said it looked like war.

King sent out a call to all corners of the nation. He asked citizens to join him in Selma for a second march to Montgomery. This march got no farther than the first one. Dr. King could not obtain a permit to demonstrate, so he turned back the marchers at the edge of town. Many who had come to march were angry that King had halted. However, he was afraid of more violence. About two weeks later, a judge approved the march and 3,000 people headed out for Montgomery on March 21. Jesse Jackson, now 23 years old, answered the call by organizing other students to travel south. They drove in a group of automobiles to Alabama.

At last Jackson came face to face with his hero, Martin Luther King, Jr. Though no one had invited him to do so, Jackson gave a speech at the gathering. His speech made quite an impression. Reporters wanted to know who that young man was. King was impressed with Jackson's speech. He was also impressed with the way Jackson moved about, taking responsibility at the march. This feeling was not shared by everyone. Andrew Young, who later became ambassador to the United Nations and the mayor of Atlanta, Georgia, remembered the way Jesse acted at the event. Young was an aide to King at the time. He said he remembers getting a little annoyed because Jesse was giving orders from the steps of Brown Chapel and nobody knew who he was. All of the other marchers came up

Montgomery police at the Alabama state capitol building, ready to confront the 1,500 marchers from Selma.

and got in line, but Jesse, assuming a staff role, automatically started directing the marchers. Young also remembered Jesse telling him what a great pamphlet Young had written. Young was flattered, and it eased the situation.

Jackson was used to people questioning his boldness when he dared to take center stage. This was how it had been back in high school and college. So it was not likely that he would change now. As always, he pressed forward. This was an opportunity he had waited for, for a long time. Now he had the chance to be seen and heard by Martin Luther King, Jr. Jackson came to admire King even more, knowing how bravely he stood against threat of death. He mentioned this when he spoke at Selma. "Dr. King was like a giant and not afraid of violence and bullets and bombs!" Jesse said.

Besides his good speech, Jackson made his mark in Selma by being willing to do any task. He even served coffee. No job was too small for him. He knew there could be more challenging ones ahead. This was something that Jackson had learned from his grandmother. There was that expression about how you have to "crawl before you can walk." There was also a line he'd heard King use in speeches. It was a line from a poem that nearly all southern black children learned: "Be the *best* of whatever you are." So regardless of the role he was playing in the movement there at Selma—whether it was coffeemaker, or messenger, or the one to dump the trash—Jackson was at his best.

Jacqueline had been unable to make the trip to Selma because she was expecting another child any day. When Jackson called home, he learned that she had given birth to their son Jonathan.

Over 50,000 people of all races and nationalities participated in the Selma march. This was one of the most important events in the whole civil rights struggle. Selma focused the attention of the media on the brutality of segregation. The media, in turn, focused the attention of the world on Selma. As a result, the Voting Rights Act became law in August 1965.

10 OPERATION BREAD-BASKET

❝ There comes a time when people get tired of being trampled over by the feet of oppression. ❞

MARTIN LUTHER KING, JR.

In 1966, Jesse Jackson began working directly with Martin Luther King, Jr. It was true that the South was the area of the country with the fewest opportunities for black people. But there was a lot of segregation in the North, too. Dr. King had made much progress in the South. But he believed a national civil rights movement was needed to change the entire United States.

The movement was at a kind of standstill because protest against the war in Vietnam was a big issue. Many of the young people who had demonstrated for civil rights were focused on the war. Yet there remained much to be done about race relations in the country.

King's opportunity to travel north came through an invitation from the Coordinating Council of Community Organizations of Chicago, or CCCO. Jackson was part of this group. He was also still working with the SCLC. The CCCO and SCLC joined forces and formed one group to deal with civil rights issues in Chicago. They called themselves the Chicago Freedom Movement. Together they pledged to work toward helping blacks find better jobs and better places to live in Chicago.

Jackson did the groundwork of organizing the local people in preparation for King's arrival. Some blacks were not anxious to get involved because they feared that the people controlling the city government would find ways to punish them. This fear was not the kind of fear that southern blacks had of people like Bull Connor. But there was still real fear. Some were afraid they would be kicked out of the public housing projects where they lived. Others thought they might lose their welfare benefits.

Jackson knew the influence that African-American preachers had on the community. He also knew that the church was a place where people could be persuaded to do the right thing. So he used the church as a base to organize black citizens.

The Reverend Clay Evans of Friendship Baptist Church offered to help. He added Jackson as youth minister to the church he led. Friendship Baptist became a center for civil rights activity in Chicago. City officials were opposed to King coming, and they were annoyed that Friendship Baptist was involved. They punished the church by denying them loan money that the church had requested. The money was supposed to go toward completing the church building. Evans stood tall and declared that the real church was in the heart of the people. "No one can stop me," he said. The work on the Friendship Baptist Church building was completed by the congregation itself. Other African-American churches were inspired by the courage of Friendship Baptist and began to take a more active role in the gatherings that Jackson organized.

When Martin Luther King, Jr., arrived in Chicago with his wife and four children, Jackson met him in a car provided by Friendship Baptist Church. The press was there in large numbers. Jackson shared the spotlight with King. King gave Jackson advice on talking to the press. This was his way to help prepare Jackson to be a leader.

King had brought his family on the trip in order to move them into one of Chicago's slum buildings. He knew that television cameras would follow him throughout his stay in the city. This would be an opportunity for the entire country to see the terrible conditions under which poor people lived in Chicago. The building King chose was dirty and had no lights in the halls. As soon as Chicago's Mayor Richard J. Daley learned that King had moved into the building, he immediately sent workers out to improve it.

King realized that he could not move to every slum apartment building to get the mayor to make improvements. So he decided that the next step would be a big rally, the kind he had held in the South. In July 1966, Jackson and King led a march from Soldier Field to City Hall. There, they presented a list of demands. The main demand was that the city open up its all-white neighborhoods to blacks. Mayor Daley offered no response.

When King decided to march into the white neighborhoods, Jackson organized things. He was able to recruit white supporters and nuns and priests to join in this effort. The march turned violent and was seen on television. Everyone was familiar with racist attitudes in the South, but the display in Chicago shocked a lot of people. Whites threw garbage and shouted racial insults at the marchers. More violence followed as whites started rioting across the city.

Mayor Daley was worried about losing the election that was

The violence at the Soldier Field Rally in Chicago became front-page news nationwide.

coming up. So he called a meeting and promised to make changes in Chicago if the protests ended and King left the city. Agreement was made to do so. Once King left, however, the mayor failed to keep his promises. Nothing changed in how the blacks lived in the city.

There were those who felt that Dr. King's trip to Chicago did not do much good. But Jesse Jackson was not among them. He had learned much from his leader. And Jackson was glad that the nation saw that there were black people in northern cities who were living in as bad conditions as the poor people in the rural South.

Before leaving the city, King appointed Jackson director of the Chicago branch of Operation Breadbasket. Operation Breadbasket was the branch of the SCLC that concentrated on finding work for poor people. Ralph Abernathy, King's assistant, said that King had named the program Operation Breadbasket because "its goal was to bring bread, money, and income into the baskets of black and poor people."

The experience in Chicago showed civil rights leaders once again that marches and sit-ins would not be enough to end segregation. They knew that economic pressure had to be used. Economic pressure had worked before—in Montgomery, when African Americans would not ride the buses, and in Albany, when African Americans stopped buying from stores. So this was the strategy of Operation Breadbasket.

King had called on Dr. Leon Sullivan, an African-American minister from Philadelphia, Pennsylvania, to help him organize the first Operation Breadbasket in Atlanta for SCLC. Sullivan had been successful in bringing about a boycott of merchants in Philadelphia. King developed plans with Jesse Jackson for the Chicago branch.

By now, Jackson's involvement with the movement had reached the point where he could not keep up with school. So he dropped out of the seminary. He very much wanted to complete his studies, but he felt that the work King had left in his charge was more important at that time. Although he did not graduate with his class, Jackson was later given an honorary degree by the same university in 1969.

Jackson, at 24 years old, was running Operation Breadbasket. He and Jackie had three children. Working with him were two white students from the seminary he had attended. The plan of Operation Breadbasket involved the following steps:

- asking blacks to buy products from black-owned companies and to shop at black-owned stores;
- asking white business that made money in black neighborhoods to hire more blacks;
- asking stores to make room on their shelves for goods made by blacks.

"Don't give our people what they need and all the blacks will stop using your products," Operation Breadbasket announced.

More than one million African Americans lived in Chicago in 1966, which meant that they spent billions of dollars in the city. But few held jobs in the places where they spent their hard-earned money. And few were returning home at night to safe, clean places to live.

Operation Breadbasket studied city businesses. It looked at businesses where blacks were spending a lot of money but no blacks worked. Country Delight, a dairy chain in Chicago, was such a company. It did a lot of business in black neighborhoods, but it had no black drivers. The word was sent out from the pulpits of more than 100 black ministers now working with Jackson. The ministers told their congregations that they should boycott the products of Country Delight. Picket lines were set up around the dairy's stores. The company hired strongmen—bullies—who tried to scare the demonstrators away. But Jackson was able to put together his own group of young men from the black neighborhoods to guard the picketers.

The dairy items spoiled quickly, so it only took three days to make the company give in and hire black workers. Forty-five people were trained to serve as drivers. The success of the Country Delight boycott was inspiration for Jackson to test other businesses that were not being fair to blacks.

The next target was the Red Rooster, a chain of supermarkets in the black community. Jackson was always willing to listen to the local people. He heard blacks from the South Side of Chicago tell horror tales about the overpriced goods and rotten meats that Red Rooster had sold to them over the years. In addition, no blacks worked in the stores. When Jackson confronted the owner of the Red Rooster, he was called a liar and an opportunist. Jackson responded, "Yes, I am an opportunist for justice—because I have taken every opportunity to try to right a wrong, whether in schools, stores, or anywhere black people are being disrespected." Operation Breadbasket's action against Red Rooster finally closed the stores down altogether in Chicago.

The Atlantic & Pacific Tea Company, better known as A&P, was the next target for a boycott. It also ended in victory for Operation Breadbasket.

Success in Chicago convinced Jackson to try the boycotts in other cities. However, he did not do as well outside of Chicago. The closeness of church and community that he was able to build in Chicago had developed over a period of time. It was not easy to move into another city and get the same kind of cooperation overnight. So he decided to stay in Chicago.

Jackson began to move Operation Breadbasket in yet another

direction. He started to urge businesses, local government offices, and ordinary citizens to put their money in black banks. He said that the banks would grow stronger this way. They would be in a position to make more loans to local black businesses. This would help improve living conditions in poor neighborhoods, Jackson said. He added that the businesses would be able to offer more college scholarships to African-American students, as soon as they were doing better. Mayor Daley did not respond to Jackson's request. But the state treasurer, Adlai Stevenson, invested city funds in two black Chicago banks.

Two other ideas sprang from Operation Breadbasket: Black Christmas and Black Easter. These programs were a celebration of the two traditional holidays, but in a different way. A community leader called on blacks to boycott downtown stores at Christmas. Jackson added that they should make sure they purchased from black businesses instead. He also called on middle-class families to invite less fortunate families into their homes for the festive days. A major parade was planned with decorated floats and displays of African-American heroes and heroines.

During 1968, Jackson learned that he had the sickle cell trait. This is a blood disease that affects African Americans of West African descent most often. He had to go to the hospital, but even there he continued his work. After his hospital stay, he returned to work at full speed. Since he didn't drink alcohol or smoke, his health was very good.

Jackson used the dining hall of the Chicago Theological Seminary for Saturday morning meetings with ministers. They discussed civil rights issues. Bankers, lawyers, and ordinary citizens gradually became part of the discussions, too. Soon, the group was too large for the dining hall and a new place had to be found.

In 1968, Jackson began holding his discussions at the Capitol Theatre on Chicago's South Side. Saturday was chosen as the day of the week for the meeting so that the gatherings would not interfere with regular Sunday church services.

The gatherings had a live band and singing from a gospel choir. Jackson spoke to the crowd about Operation Breadbasket and inspired it to carry on the struggle. "Everybody went," one woman says of the meetings. "For one reason or another, it was the place to be. Some went to get spiritual uplifting, others went to take part in the boycotts or just to see a friend. Some Saturdays the place was so jammed, there was standing room only. You'd have to get there early or you didn't get a seat." Those who were not able to attend could hear the program on the radio.

"I *am somebody*!" Jackson shouted out and asked the audience to repeat. "I *am* somebody!" the people chanted back. He would go on to remind them of the fine tradition from which the African-American race had come. As he quoted ideas and passages he had read from great African-American thinkers such as W. E. B. Du Bois, Jackson told them of their strength as a people. Jackson dressed casually and had his hair cut in the huge Afro hairstyle nearly all young blacks of the day wore. He was a striking and charming figure, growing more popular with the crowd each week.

Again, his popularity stirred up jealousy and complaints. There were people who said his organization used pressure on companies to hire members of Chicago youth gangs. Jackson saw this as a way of getting the young people involved and off the street. But there were complaints that the gang members were not doing their work well and that the merchants were afraid of them. There always seemed to be someone complaining. People were not only complaining about Jackson trying to help the young gangs who were poor. There were also complaints that he was helping rich black businessmen too much. Some went so far as to say that the only people getting anything out of the boycotts were rich black businessmen who had become friends of Jesse Jackson.

Jackson understood that no movement could be without criticism. So he accepted whatever questions came his way. All that he could do was continue his work. And there was plenty of work to be done. Much of the hope that African Americans had had for social and economic changes in the country died with the assassination of President John F. Kennedy. It had been Kennedy's dream to put many new programs in place that would benefit minority groups. But his dream was cut short when he was shot down in Dallas, Texas, in November 1963.

President Kennedy was succeeded by President Lyndon B. Johnson. Johnson was the president who finally signed the Civil Rights Act in 1964 and the Voting Rights Act in 1965. Many of President Kennedy's ideas for social programs were carried through by President Johnson. These programs tried to eliminate poverty and hunger. Johnson called his programs the War on Poverty and the Great Society. Congress passed laws setting up job training programs and raising the minimum wage. Project Head Start provided learning programs for preschool children. A housing act helped poor families pay their rent and also find housing. Congress also began federal health insurance programs for older people and for those with disabilities or low incomes. These programs helped millions of Americans including African Americans.

But what was not good for them, or for the whole country during the Johnson administration, was the war in Vietnam. Thousands of young soldiers were killed during the war. There was a larger percentage of blacks sent into battle than whites. Martin Luther King, Jr., spoke out against the war. King felt that black soldiers were fighting for their country, but they were still denied their full rights as citizens. Jackson raised his voice, too. Malcolm X, before his assassination in 1965, also spoke about young black men having to serve in Vietnam. Many young white men whose families had money to send them away to college were able to stay out of the war. Malcolm X called attention to this. He often made this kind of bold public statement. Although Malcolm X was shot by black men, many people today believe that there were others who wanted Malcolm X dead. After his death, there was growing anger among young blacks. They shouted as Stokely Carmichael had, "Black Power!"

Stokely's slogan was first announced in 1966. Shortly after that, two young black men in Oakland, California—Huey Newton and Bobby Seale—started what was known as the Black Panther party. An unorganized riot had taken place in the city of Oakland. There was stealing and destruction of property. Many blacks were showing the frustrations they felt about poverty, unemployment, and the poor conditions where they lived. The riot left their neighborhood in worse shape than it had been. Through the use of extra police, city officials tried to bring calm. Instead, more confusion resulted. Huey Newton and Bobby Seale created their program in an effort to bring some organization to the community. They felt that the young people needed direction.

Both King and Jackson made a prediction. They both said that unless better opportunities were given to poor young people in America, separatist groups such as the Black Panthers would increase. This was why Jackson had wanted to bring the young gang members into the work of Operation Breadbasket in Chicago. It was better, he felt, to have the youths inside the movement where their energies and skills would be used for the good of all. And again, Jackson felt that they, too, needed to be offered a chance to change their lives for the better. They should not remain victims of racism, he felt. For as Jesse said:

> Racism is unproductive economically.
> Racism is unhealthy and sick.
> Racism is immoral.
> Racism has made us less credible as a people.
> We must reject racism.

Jesse believed, as Martin Luther King, Jr., taught, that we would "learn to live together as brothers and sisters (in America) or surely die apart as fools."

11 TROUBLING TIMES FOR THE MOVEMENT

> **❝** *We must have the moral courage to stand up and protest against injustice wherever we find it.* **❞**

MARTIN LUTHER KING, JR.

In 1967, the SCLC began planning another major march on Washington. The aim of the march was to bring the country's attention to the plight of poor people—black and white. Martin Luther King, Jr., wanted the government to turn its attention to their needs. The great March on Washington of 1963 had been so powerful that he planned to pattern the next march after that one. Jesse Jackson began working with the SCLC people in Atlanta on the project. Plans were interrupted when King was called to Memphis, Tennessee, to assist in a crisis there. His aides begged him not to go. They said that all of his energies were needed for the Poor People's March to Washington.

But the situation in Memphis was so serious that King felt he could not help but become involved. Two black sanitation workers had been accidentally crushed to death in a garbage truck. Their deaths were the result of a racist act by white co-workers. The two black men had stood beneath the truck seeking shelter from a heavy downpour of rain. They had not been allowed to stay inside the garbage truck with the white workers. The deaths of the two black men came about because they were denied a privilege as simple as standing in a dry place out of the rain.

A protest march was organized by black garbage workers. On March 28, 1968, King arrived in Memphis to lead the march through town. The march turned violent, and King's aides quickly pulled him from the crowd. King was very upset about the way the march had turned out. It was learned years later that the two young black men who had started the violence had been paid by enemies of the movement.

Because King was speaking out against the war in Vietnam, he had new enemies. By now the Federal Bureau of Investigation (FBI) was spying on all of his activities. The FBI did not want to see King continue to be the powerful leader that he was. So the FBI paid people money to be disruptive and start confusion, as they did in Memphis. This, the FBI hoped, would damage Dr. King's leadership.

Martin Luther King, Jr., had been awarded the Nobel Peace Prize on December 10, 1964. Even the FBI knew that he was a major leader—not only in this country, but abroad. J. Edgar Hoover, the head of the FBI, did not admire King. He did not trust him and worked hard at trying to discredit him. He even tried to convince people in the government that King was a Communist who was out to do the United States harm.

In spite of this setback, King was determined to stay in Memphis and continue to speak on behalf of the black sanita-

Jackson stands with Dr. Martin Luther King, Jr., hours
before King is killed on the same balcony.

tion workers. Jesse Jackson, Andrew Young, Ralph Abernathy,
Hosea Williams, and other aides remained with him there.

On April 3, King spoke to a crowd at a local Baptist church.
He told them he may not reach "the Promised Land" with
them, but that someday they would all be free. King was convinced that the day would come when all the dreams of equality
for blacks that he had struggled for would come about.

The following day King spent planning the next step of the
Memphis protest. That evening King, his staff, and aides were
preparing to go to dinner at the home of a local pastor. King and
the older men always wore suits and ties to dinner. Jesse Jackson
and the younger generation dressed more casually. That evening, King kidded Jackson about the casual clothes that he was
wearing. King was standing on the balcony of the Lorraine
Motel where the group was staying. He asked a musician with

Jesse Jackson holds a copy of a newspaper announcing the death of Dr. King.

Jackson if, later that night, he would play his favorite song, "Precious Lord Lead Me On." It was six o'clock—time for dinner. Suddenly a shot rang out. The target was King, and the bullet struck him down. Ralph Abernathy rushed from the motel room to his friend's side. There was terrible confusion. People rushed around trying to get help.

The doctors at the hospital did what they could. Martin Luther King, Jr., died an hour after he was shot.

Jackson appeared on television the following morning saying that he was the last person to speak to King. Many who were there disagree. Others say that the confusion of the moment may have made the order of events appear this way to him.

The night that Martin Luther King, Jr., was shot, black youths rioted in cities across the country. Jackson immediately returned to Chicago. There, he became a peacemaker. He helped quiet down the violence that was spreading among blacks. "I am calling for nonviolence in the homes, on the streets, in the classrooms, and in our relationship with one another," he said. "I'm challenging the youth of today to be nonviolent as the greatest expression of faith they can make in King—Put your rocks down, put your bottles down."

Mayor Daley was worried. He called a special session of the city council to honor King. Jesse Jackson addressed the crowd wearing the same blood-stained clothes he had left Memphis in the day before. He had worn the same clothes on the NBC "Today" show as well. Jackson used the moment with the city council to remind Mayor Daley and other officials of how poorly they had treated Dr. King when he had come to the city. He ended by letting them know that the best tribute they could pay to the fallen leader was to change their ways. "This would mean more than sitting and looking sad," Jesse told them.

More than 4,000 people came to the Martin Luther King, Jr., memorial service held the next Saturday morning at the Capitol Theatre. Jackson spoke not only of the loss to African Americans in the death of King, but also of the loss to the whole nation. And he told of the need to keep fighting for all that King stood for. He recalled specific words of his hero: "Don't stop now. Keep moving. Walk together, children."

The Poor People's March that King had planned did take place. Ralph Abernathy took over for King. But for many reasons, including poor leadership, it did not go well. In planning the event, no one had thought of the possibility that there might be bad weather. The plan was that all of those who traveled to Washington were to camp outside at a site called Resurrection City. Many of the leaders chose hotels, however, leaving the so-called grassroots people behind. Tempers were bad because of the rain, and arguments began. Jackson was named "City Manager" of Resurrection City by Ralph Abernathy. When he arrived, he was able to bring some calm to the muddled affair by asking troublemakers to leave. But overall, the Poor People's March was not looked upon as a successful event. This was the first major event for Ralph Abernathy since King's death. And it was not good for his record as a new leader.

Shortly thereafter, Jackson became a minister. The man who ordained him was the Reverend C. E. Franklin, the father of the famous singer Aretha Franklin. Through Aretha Franklin, Jackson came to know other entertainment figures.

He still wore his large Afro hairstyle. He liked to wear dashikis (African shirts), turtlenecks, leather vests, and bell-bottomed pants. Around his neck, he wore a huge medallion of Dr. King.

When Jackson stood before his Saturday morning crowds, he appealed to young and old. He was a perfect mix of good country preacher and smooth city boy. Everybody liked him. He knew how to work an audience, as the old people down South used to say.

As his popularity grew, so did the jealousy of him by other black leaders. There was growing friction between Jesse Jackson and Ralph Abernathy, then the official leader of the SCLC. Abernathy had been chosen to replace King by King himself. But the press announced Jackson as the new black leader. *Time* magazine even did a cover story on Jackson. At age 29, Jackson was the youngest black man ever to have that honor.

In 1970, the first Black Expo was held in Chicago through Operation Breadbasket. Proceeds were to go to the SCLC. The idea of the Black Expo was to have business people gather at a kind of convention where ideas could be exchanged. There would also be entertainment. Friends that Jackson had made, such as Aretha Franklin, the Jackson Five, and Nancy Wilson, provided free entertainment for the Black Expo. The success of the gathering brought Jackson even more fame. And it stirred more jealousy among SCLC members too. They felt he was getting too much attention. By the time that the next Black Expo began, the situation had gotten worse.

In 1971, Jackson resigned from Operation Breadbasket and the Southern Christian Leadership Conference. There was too much tension between his Chicago office of Operation Breadbasket and the Atlanta staff of the SCLC. Questions were asked about money that was raised in the SCLC's name but that never reached the organization. After examining all the records of Operation Breadbasket, the SCLC decided the program was honest.

When followers of Jackson learned that he had resigned from the SCLC, they let him know that they were behind him. They said that they were willing to give their help to launch any ideas he might have. Jackson was encouraged by their support. He formed a new organization and named it Operation PUSH. In the beginning PUSH stood for People United to Save Humanity. One of the founding ministers suggested that "serve" sounded better because humanity could not be saved by mere humans. So PUSH changed its name.

The Saturday morning meetings, including the band, choir, and audience, left the SCLC with Jackson. But much of the financial backing that he had developed in the business community stayed behind. PUSH purchased its own building, and the Saturday meetings continued.

The goals of PUSH were the same as those of Operation Breadbasket. PUSH too aimed for better jobs, quality health care, and improvements in education. A lot of attention was focused on the growth of black businesses. Businesses were asked to see that blacks were able to buy and operate their stores. Large distributors such as Coca-Cola were questioned on their policies regarding blacks. Many of the companies began to see the need to respond favorably. They knew that black people were their customers, too.

In 1973, Jesse Jackson's hometown of Greenville, South Carolina, officially welcomed him home. By now he had been on

many television shows. He had also been on the covers of magazines and had received several honorary degrees. For Jackson, this trip back home was one of his proudest moments.

Signs were up all over town welcoming him home. The local paper carried a full-page greeting saying, "Here Comes the Son." Friends, family, and old school friends were there. Jackson was deeply moved by the celebration. It was one of the proudest days of his life. Even so, he let the people know that there was more work to be done.

TOWARD YOUTH AND THE FUTURE

> **Boys can make a baby. Taking care of that baby, providing love and family stability is what makes you a man.**
>
> **JESSE JACKSON**

PUSH was making a lot of progress in helping many blacks to own their own businesses. Nevertheless, criticism of the organization continued. There were still people who insisted that the program was only helping upper-income people. Some of the criticism was from people who were jealous of Jackson and wanted to see him brought down in some way. He was moving in large political groups, and critics wanted to find a way to make him less popular. Jackson recognized this as political jealousy. He also realized that it was time for PUSH to move in new directions. Jackson studied the situation. Then he fasted and prayed, the way many spiritual leaders do when they are looking for guidance or solutions to problems. In time, he decided that PUSH should focus on youth. The organization would seek ways of helping young people solve some of the problems they were facing.

There was an important reason why Jackson came to this decision. On January 15, 1974, Martin Luther King, Jr.'s, birthday, Jackson had led a march in Washington to focus on joblessness in the country. He noticed that many young people kept dropping out of the march because they got tired. He was upset when he learned that some of them were on drugs. He noted that more and more young people were on the Chicago streets during the day when they should have been in school.

Jackson also noticed that larger numbers of teenage girls were getting pregnant. These realizations helped him to make his decision for the new direction of PUSH. The organization should shift its focus from the business world for a while, he decided. It would begin to address the problems of youths.

First of all, young people needed to understand how important it was for them to get a good education. Skills with computers and other new technologies would be needed to compete for jobs in the future. There would be no place for people without good training. Teenagers also needed to understand the evil of drugs. Jackson wanted to let them know that the dealers who brought drugs into their communities were their enemies. And finally, he felt that someone had to speak out on the loss of moral values. For example, some teenagers now used foul language in the presence of adults. Jackson knew that it had not always been this way. At least it had not been this way in his community. Jackson told his audiences that in the past no child would ever curse in front of an adult. They respected their elders too much.

Another thing disturbed him, too. This was the lack of racial pride some young people showed. African Americans had fought and died in the protest against *not* being respected. Yet there were some black teenagers who openly used negative words like *nigger* in public conversations. All of this needed to change. Jackson had to find a way to reach his young audiences. It was time for young people to return to the pride and principles that their forefathers and mothers lived by.

Jackson chose the name EXCEL for his new program. It was a short name for EXCELLENCE. Then he challenged youths. He asked them to strive for excellence in all that they did—from their schoolwork to their self-respect.

Jackson traveled across the country to speak in the EXCEL program. He stood before his audience looking polished and professional in a neat business suit and tie. The late 1970s brought a new style of dress for him. He was older, and he moved in political and business circles. So he dressed more like a businessman. Like most proud African Americans, he still wore a "natural" hairstyle, but it was now cut in a shorter and more modern fashion. The huge Afro he and young people had worn to express racial pride in the 1960s was cut shorter. Jackson's turtlenecks, vests, and even his African dashikis that were so popular during the sixties remained part of his wardrobe. But his new style of clothing had its own place in his life. Just as his mother and grandmother had imposed what were called Sunday clothes and shoes, back when he was growing up, Jackson had what one might call special public clothes now.

As he faced his teenage audiences, Jackson began by telling them how special they were. Then he told them how they could improve their lives. "Work hard and strive for excellence," he advised. "You may be in the slums, but don't let the slum be in you." Then Jackson called out and asked the students to recite line for line after him:

"I am somebody.
I may be poor,
but I am somebody!

I may be poorly educated,
but I am somebody!
I may be on welfare,
I may be prematurely pregnant,
I may be on drugs,
I may be victimized by racism,
but I am somebody!
Respect me. Protect me. Never neglect me.
I am God's child."

At each school, he asked students to sign a contract pledging to stay away from drugs and alcohol and to study two hours each night. He challenged parents to become more involved in their children's lives at school and at home. He also asked teachers to pledge to have more communication with parents.

Jackson had a special style of talking, or "rapping," as young people called it. He became famous for what is known in the black community as "signifying." To signify is to be hip or cool in your conversation. Words take on new meanings. Sometimes they rhyme. When Jesse Jackson spoke, he preached and recited poetry.

When the storms of life rage and our enemies mount
    against us, we must use willpower, and not pill power.
Hold your heads high!
Just because it rains, we don't have to drown!
Hold your heads high!
When it's dark out, the stars can be seen most clearly.
Hold your heads high!
We are victims of second-class treatment, but we are first-
    class people.
God has space for us, a time and place for us!
Through it all, we've learned to trust him! Our burden is
    heavy, our suffering is great.

But God is the source of energy.
He didn't bring us this far to leave us!

Speaking before a group of youth in Atlanta, Georgia at a Teen Conference in 1978, Jackson said:

> Every now and then I hear young people brag about the new generation. It's not really anything to brag about because you didn't do anything to become the new generation. Your parents did something to make the new generation. You are the new generation without effort. So why brag about being *new* when it's not the result of your work? Why brag about being black or white? It's not the result of your work. Your challenge is to become a greater generation. And you become a greater generation because you serve. If you feed more hungry people, you are a greater generation. If more people of this generation are educated, it's a greater generation. If the racial lines that separate us are overcome, you are a greater generation. And so our challenge is to be not just a new generation, based on birth, but to be a greater generation based upon work and effort.
>
> There's always the challenge of concentration. We used to have a saying some years ago in the freedom struggle, "Keep your eyes on the prize." If your prize is to develop your mind; if your prize is to develop your body; if your prize is to develop spiritual depth; if your prize is to grow up healthy, marry, and develop a family—if that is your prize, then don't let any activity divert you from your prize. When we are traveling, sometimes there are bumps in the road. Sometimes there are potholes in the road. Sometimes nails and broken glass may puncture our tire and delay us and divert us from the prize. Keep your eyes on the prize.

Young people always listen well when Jesse Jackson speaks. But he once told a story about how he had difficulty getting a young man's attention when Jackson wanted him to remove his hat inside a building. The young man was giving Jackson a hard time. When questioned about his hat, the student responded that it made no difference what was on his head. What mattered was what was inside of it. Jackson listened patiently, nodding his head as the young man spoke. Then he told the student that what he said might be true. But if he were going for a job interview and did not remove his hat, no one would bother to find out what lay inside his skull! At that point, the boy promptly took off the hat.

Jackson also had a special message for athletes. Wherever he traveled, he let high school stars know that it is important not to depend totally on a sports career. No one can depend on sports as a means of support for his or her entire adult life, he declared.

Some young black athletes weren't able to graduate from college. EXCEL began studying how the program might help these athletes. Jackson's background enabled him to convince young athletes that they could have both physical and mental excellence. He was the perfect example.

There are visible results of Jackson's efforts with EXCEL. Grades have risen and remained higher in many of the schools following Jesse's visits. Students in Los Angeles decided to make their school be number one in academics as well as sports. Students in Missouri school raised money to make their building more beautiful. In Chicago, students stopped skipping classes at a school he visited. Some schools have started branches of EXCEL for themselves.

In 1977, EXCEL was highlighted on the "60 Minutes" television program. The late Senator Hubert Humphrey was so impressed that he asked the head of the U.S. Department of Education to give Jackson a grant. This helped Jackson take the EXCEL program into more schools.

The work of the EXCEL program continues today, as does PUSH. The organization's main effort is to improve the lives of the poor and minorities. Through PUSH, Jackson took a group of congresspeople to Tunica, Mississippi, the poorest place in the country. In Tunica, people still lived without indoor toilets or water in the 1980s. Nearly all the citizens of Tunica were black. They suffered from desperate poverty. Few of them could read or write. Since the visit by Jackson and the congresspeople, conditions have been improved for the poor people of Tunica. This has become Jackson's style over the years. He travels directly to a place so that he can know a situation firsthand.

Throughout the late 1970s, Jackson spent considerable time traveling to foreign countries. His first major trip was to Africa. He went to Lagos, Nigeria, where he attended a cultural festival. When he returned, Jackson told black people how important it was for him to make this trip. He has led drives to aid in the droughts in West Africa. He also took African-American businessman to Liberia. They discussed opening businesses there and Liberians opening businesses in this country. Jackson has strongly denounced apartheid. (Apartheid is a system of government in South Africa that separates the races. It keeps blacks living at a lower standard than whites.) When Jackson arrived in South Africa, he was greeted by blacks with a banner that read, "Welcome Reverend Jesse Jackson, distinguished son of Mother Africa." He told his African sisters and brothers that there were people in the United States who supported their struggle for equality.

Jackson also spent time in the Middle East, where he visited Israel, Lebanon, Syria, Jordan, and Egypt. He visited and met with Fidel Castro, the leader of Cuba. His trips to Europe included visits to U.S. military bases. At the bases, he spoke with American servicemen and women and their families. The purpose of all of his travels was to get a better understanding of different parts of the world.

As he traveled abroad and around the United States, Jackson began to see that there was a close relationship between economics and politics. All the social programs that he wanted for the country required money—money that was tied to government decisions. He felt he needed to be involved in politics.

In 1972, at age 30, he surprised people around him by suddenly deciding to run for mayor of Chicago. People were puzzled. There was no way he could win against the powerful Mayor Daley. Jackson realized this, too. But he understood the importance of minority people realizing that they *could* run— even against someone as powerful as the mayor of Chicago. Jackson did poorly in the race, but he proved his courage by running.

Jackson faced Daley again in 1972 in another challenge. It was not to run as mayor, however. At the 1972 Democratic Convention, Jackson challenged the way Mayor Daley had selected Illinois delegates for the convention. The rules said that selection should be made in an open meeting. But Mayor Daley had made his pick in secret. Hardly any blacks were included. After Jackson took the matter before the Democratic National Convention Credentials Committee, Mayor Daley's people had to leave. An open vote took place, and a new slate of delegates was elected.

August 28, 1983, marked the twentieth anniversary of the civil rights March on Washington. Speaking on the occasion Jackson said, "Twenty years later, we have our freedom—our civil rights. But twenty years later, we still do not have equality. We have moved in. Now we must move up."

JESSE JACKSON AND THE RAINBOW COALITION

> *We have a great nation, but it can be greater if all Americans are included.*
>
> **MARTIN LUTHER KING, JR.**

In November 1983, Jesse Louis Jackson made the official announcement that he would seek the Democratic party's nomination for the presidency of the United States. He called his backers the Rainbow Coalition. The group included the "left-outs," he said. "Blacks, poor whites, women, Hispanics, Arabs, Asians, and Native Americans. Red, yellow, black and white—we're all precious in God's sight!"

Seven other candidates also wanted the democratic nomination. All of them had more money to work with than Jesse

Jackson. The left-outs who backed Jackson could contribute little or no money to support their candidate.

There had been questions when Jesse had dared to run for mayor of Chicago. Now people were asking why once again. Jackson's response was, "If you run, you may lose, but if you don't run, you're guaranteed to lose!"

And so the Rainbow Coalition was on its way. Its numbers grew as other left-out groups—such as farmers who had lost their farms—joined the coalition.

Support was slow in coming from important black leaders—especially those still loyal to Ralph Abernathy and the SCLC. Among those was Coretta Scott King, Dr. King's widow. She was head of the Center for Research and Social Change in Atlanta, Georgia. This group still felt that Jackson had taken power from the SCLC with his PUSH organization. It did not come out and say this, however. Instead, it said it was concerned that Jackson would take votes away from Walter Mondale, the leading moderate white candidate. Other black civil rights figures and politicians were convinced that it was more practical to get behind Mondale.

Mondale, they believed, had some chance of winning over the conservative Republican then in office. The Republicans, led by Ronald Reagan, had done little for civil rights. Jackson's black opponents said that minorities should help get a Democrat into the White House. Walter Mondale was thought to be the best person.

One supporter of Jesse Jackson was Mayor Richard Hatcher of Gary, Indiana. Mayor Hatcher became national chairperson of the Jesse Jackson for President Committee. He spoke to the press and to Jackson supporters on July 15, the night before the opening of the national Democratic Convention in San Francisco. "I am so happy that years from now when my children and grandchildren study the history books and say to me, 'Grandaddy, tell me about this man Jesse Jackson. Where were you when he ran for president? Did you help him?' I am so happy tonight because I will be able to say, 'Yes, I knew Jesse Jackson. I stood right with him and did all I could to help his great crusade.' I am so happy that I will not have to give excuses," Hatcher said. "Yes, I will be proud to tell my children and grandchildren that their grandaddy was on the right side of history. . . ."

Mayor Hatcher was not alone. Other leading black politicians decided to join with Jesse Jackson and the Rainbow Coalition. They agreed with the cry that Jackson should be chosen for minorities and other left-out people in America. This was the cry of "Our Time Has Come."

Just as when he ran for mayor of Chicago, Jackson understood that he might not win. But still, he saw the need to enter the race at that particular time. For he saw the pain and frustration of those who could not help themselves—the poor, the homeless, the uneducated. Jesse was ready to lift up their cause.

The title of his announcement speech for the Democratic nomination was "The Quest for a Just Society." Speaking at the Washington Convention Center in the District of Columbia on November 3, 1983, he said:

> I offer myself to the American people . . . as a vehicle to give a voice to the voiceless, representation to the unrepresented and hope to the downtrodden. . . .
>
> Lest there be confusion, let the word go forth from this occasion that this candidacy is not for blacks only. This is a national campaign growing out of the black experience seen through the eyes of a black perspective—which is the experience and perspective of the rejected. Because of this experience, I can empathize with the plight of Appalachia because I have known poverty. I know the pain of anti-Semitism because I have felt the humiliation of discrimination. I know firsthand the shame of bread lines and the horror of hopelessness and despair because my life had

been dedicated to empowering the world's rejected to become respected. I would like to use this candidacy to help build a new rainbow coalition of the rejected that will include whites, blacks, Hispanics, Indians, and Native Americans, Asians, women, young people, poor people, old persons, peace activists and environmentalists. If we remain separated, we will forever remain poor and powerless. But if we come together...we won't be poor and powerless anymore.

Jesse Jackson went on to say that as a candidate, he would offer new leadership. He would defend the poor. He would seek to bring peace in the world and make sure there would be justice for all people.

Just as he launched his campaign, a black U.S. Navy airman was shot down over Lebanon. His name was Lieutenant Robert O. Goodman. Goodman was taken as a prisoner of war.

Jackson traveled to Syria to seek his release. American politicians and the press objected to his trip. They felt that Jesse Jackson had no business doing this as an ordinary citizen. But then, Jackson did not view himself as an ordinary citizen. He was a presidential candidate, and he had a good relationship with the Arab world. Jackson felt he had a responsibility to help Lieutenant Goodman.

The State Department did not approve of the trip. So Jackson traveled completely at his own risk. He returned with Goodman and was a hero to the nation. President Reagan had been critical of Jackson prior to the trip. But when they got back, the president invited him and the airman to visit the White House. Jesse Jackson made it clear to the press that his purpose had not been to return a hero. He had simply wanted to help free Lieutenant Goodman. Jackson stated, "Whoever has the courage to act, should act."

Jackson got a lot of good newspaper coverage from the Goodman victory. But bad press came from an incident that occurred

Minister Louis Farrakhan, the head of the Nation of Islam.

shortly afterward. A black newspaper reporter said that Jesse Jackson had referred to New York City, a city where many Jews live, as "Hymietown." This expression was a racial slur, and it caused anger among Jews. Jackson apologized for making the comment, but his apology did not end the criticism.

A second incident caused more bad press. This incident arose because of Jackson's association with Louis Farrakhan, a Muslim religious leader. Farrakhan was one of the black leaders who supported Jackson's announcement to run for the presidency early on. Farrakhan had learned that there had been threats on Jackson's life. Farrakhan had witnessed the assassination of many black leaders who spoke out for justice. He and his group decided to offer protection to Jackson in the form of bodyguards. The government gave protection to all presidential candidates, but Farrakhan and his followers wanted Jesse Jackson to have additional support. So they began to travel with him in small numbers as he campaigned.

After Jackson's "Hymietown" remark, strong word came from a militant Jewish group. They were called the Jewish Defense League, or JDL. The JDL was not pleased with Jesse Jackson seeking the presidency. Jackson had said that the Arab world should be given a greater voice in the Middle East disputes. The JDL did not agree. Jews and Arabs were in conflict in the Middle East. Jackson's Middle East position raised even more concern among many Jews than did his "Hymietown" remark. Around this time, Farrakhan was reported to have made a very negative comment about the Jewish faith. He called it a gutter religion.

Cries came from both blacks and whites across the country. Jackson was called upon to distance himself from Farrakhan. Jackson said he felt bad that such a statement had been made, but he would not turn his back on a man who had given him friendship and support.

During his speech at the Democratic National Convention on July 17, 1984, Jackson tried to clear away the resentment over his "Hymietown" statement. He said:

> If in my low moments, in word, deed, or attitude, some error of temper, taste, or tone, I have caused anyone discomfort, created pain, or revived someone's fears, that was not my truest self... please forgive me. Charge it to my head, and not to my heart....

> This campaign has taught me much; that leaders must be tough enough to fight, tender enough to cry, human enough to absorb the pain, and resilient enough to bounce back and keep on moving.

> For leaders, the pain is often intense. But you must smile through your tears and keep moving with the faith that there is a brighter side somewhere...

Walter Mondale won the Democratic nomination for president in 1984. Jesse Jackson's speech, however, will long be remembered. He stirred memories of King's speeches. Jackson placed these challenges before America:

> I just want young America to do me one favor—just one favor. Exercise the right to dream. You must face reality— that which is; but then dream of the reality that ought to be. Live beyond the pain of the reality with the dream of a bright tomorrow. Use hope and imagination as weapons of survival and progress. Use love to motivate you and obligate you to serve the human family.
>
> Young America, dream. Choose the human race over the nuclear race. Bury the weapons and don't burn the people. Dream—dream of a new value system. Teachers who teach for a life and not just a living; teach because they can't help it. Dream of lawyers more concerned about justice than a judgeship. Dream of doctors more concerned about public health than personal wealth. Dream of preachers who will prophesy and not just profiteer. Preach and dream! Our time has come. Our time has come.
>
> Our time has come. No grave can hold our body down.
>
> Our time has come. No lie can live forever. Our time has come. We must leave the racial battleground and find the economic common ground and moral higher ground. America, our time has come.

Jackson had seen some success in this campaign, even though he did not win the Democratic nomination. He actually won the primary election in Washington, D.C. But the most important thing that he did was to open up the door for the next time. Next time he would do even better.

JACKSON RUNS AGAIN

We cannot be satisfied as long as the Negro in Mississippi cannot vote and a Negro in New York believes he has nothing to vote for.

MARTIN LUTHER KING, JR.

Jackson did not come away from the Democratic National Convention completely satisfied. There were issues on which he had wanted the Democratic party to take a stronger stand. One of these was the issue of South Africa. He felt that the United States should be playing a bigger role in helping to end the unfair system of apartheid. Jackson was not happy about the final list of issues that the Democrats said they would push. Nevertheless, he still supported the party's choice, Walter Mondale. But the Democrats' candidate lost. President Ronald Reagan was re-elected president.

Jesse Jackson's 1988 Campaign for President of the United States

In 1988, Jesse Jackson ran a second time seeking the Democratic nomination as candidate for the office of president of the United States. Throughout the primary elections, he was among the top three Democratic candidates. At one point he was even in the lead. Jesse Jackson's political organization, the Rainbow Coalition, gave voice to many groups who felt left out of the political system. The race among the three candidates continued all the way up until the Democratic National Convention. However, Jesse Jackson's support was finally not enough to get him nominated as the Democratic candidate for president.

Jackson visits with children at a public housing project in Cleveland during his campaign for president.

Jesse Jackson and his family stand before a cheering audience after his speech at the Democratic National Convention.

Jackson brings Rosa Parks to the podium of the 1988 Democratic National Convention. This is a TV picture. Millions of Americans watched Jackson on TV.

Jesse Jackson '88

Jackson's supporters at the 1988 Democratic Convention cheer him on.

Jackson was not happy with the re-election of Reagan. He saw four more years of a government that showed little concern for the poor and minorities. So he felt his work as a spokesperson in this country had to go on. He continued to speak out on the need for improvements in housing, education, health care, reduction in military spending, and issues of the environment. In addition to speaking on the need for change in America, he stressed the urgency of the need for peace in the Middle East and an end to apartheid in South Africa.

Through PUSH he addressed young people directly. With the rising problems of drugs and teenage pregnancy, Jackson made more time to speak with young audiences.

He asked young people to think about the word for drugs, DOPE. "Why do they call it that?" he would ask. "You don't have to take drugs. You make the choice...why not choose life over death? Down with dope. Up with hope!"

He told them how important it was to study hard and stay in school. Jackson called on students to think of their brains as precious jewels. "Say, my mind is a pearl, I can learn anything in this world!" he would tell them.

Jackson appeared on television shows to play himself. He gave students in the make-believe television programs the same lesson that he gave real student audiences.

After Jackson ran for president, the press watched his activities closely. Questions came up about where the PUSH operation got its money. The government examined the organization's taxes. In the end, PUSH had to pay some money to the government, but there was no proof of any wrongdoing.

Jesse Jackson remained a very public figure between 1984 and 1987. Whenever the opportunity presented itself, he spoke out on the direction in which he felt the country should be moving. This led many to believe that he was still very much interested in being president. In 1987, Jackson announced that he would run for president a second time.

Jackson had to compete against six other candidates. The press said that he was the best known of all candidates, but it also stated that it was not likely that he would win. Jackson scored high in popularity polls taken around the country by newspapers and television. But the media people continued to suggest that a black person could not win. They still felt that there would not be enough support from voters who were not black.

But times were changing. The Rainbow Coalition was growing. Most of the African-American leaders who had not had faith in Jackson the first time he ran were behind him this time. They could not deny his strength as a candidate. Then more support came from others. Many middle-income whites recognized that government cutbacks had badly affected their lives. So they too joined the crowds shouting, "Run, Jesse, run!"

Jackson campaigned hard, visiting as many cities as he could. Many people who had not previously voted now registered to vote because of him. There were many elderly blacks who said that they had wanted the opportunity to vote for a black candidate in their lifetime. And there were young people, too, who were inspired to vote because Jackson was a candidate.

Soon, Senator Albert Gore of Tennessee and Governor Michael Dukakis of Massachusetts became the two Democratic front-runners, with Jackson following them. Then came Super Tuesday, March 8, 1988, the day when 20 southern states all held their Democratic primaries. On Super Tuesday, Jesse made a good showing. The three front-runners for the Democratic nomination then were Gore, Jackson, and Dukakis. Jackson had moved up in the vote ranking.

Reporters felt that Jackson had done well in the South because of the black vote. They said he would probably not come out as well in other parts of the country. Their prediction was wrong, however. Jackson won in Michigan, a northern state. The Michigan victory gave him 646 delegates. (Delegates are the persons needed to help place a candidate's name in nomination for the presidency.) Dukakis then had 653 delegates, and Gore, 381. Jackson was ahead!

The time was nearing for the primary contest in New York State. Once again press stories came up about Jackson's calling New York City "Hymietown." New York City's Jewish mayor, Edward I. Koch, said that Jews would be foolish to vote for Jesse Jackson. This angered blacks and many Jews as well. No one wanted to see black and Jewish relationships strained again. In spite of Koch's comments, Jackson received a large share of the votes. But Dukakis won the New York State primary.

Dukakis continued to be the leading candidate. Jackson had a strong second showing. Black political leaders across the country were saying that if Jackson were white, he would probably be considered for vice president. But no such offer came from the Democratic party. Jackson did not let this slow him down. He continued to campaign—for himself and for the ideas of the Democratic party.

The Republican party's leader, President Ronald Reagan, was at the end of his second term. He had served for as many years as the Constitution of the United States allowed. The candidate that the Republicans favored was Reagan's vice president, George Bush. The Republican Convention took place in New Orleans. As expected, George Bush was named as the Republicans' choice.

The Democratic National Convention took place in Atlanta, Georgia. Michael Dukakis was named the Democrats' candidate. Dukakis was supposed to be the main attraction of the Democratic Convention. But the crowd's excitement was greatest the night before Dukakis was to speak. This was the night that Jesse Jackson was scheduled to speak. Many Americans recalled how powerful Jackson's speech had been in 1984, and they were eager to hear him again.

He addressed the Democratic National Convention on July 19, 1988. His five children introduced Jackson. He called them

"The Jackson Five." When he came on stage, Jackson brought with him Rosa Parks, who received a standing ovation from the crowd.

In his speech to the convention, Jackson praised Parks for her work in the civil rights movement during the 1950s and 1960s. He also praised the people who had made it possible for him, an African American, to run for president. He said that his right and privilege to stand before a national audience had been won by those who had struggled, and some who had died, in the civil rights movement.

Among those he mentioned were Fannie Lou Hamer, the poor black sharecropper who had been beaten and jailed in Mississippi for helping people register to vote. She had also helped form the Mississippi Freedom Democratic Party in 1964. But the MFDP had not been allowed to take its place in the Democratic National Convention in 1964. Jackson also named Viola Liuzzo. She was a white woman from Detroit who had been killed giving a ride to black people demonstrating for voter rights in Alabama. He named Michael Schwerner, Andrew Goodman, and James Chaney—two Jews and a black who were killed in Mississippi as they worked in the Freedom Project. And Jackson could not forget the four little black girls, Denise, Cynthia, Carol, and Addie Mae. They were killed in a fire-bomb attack on their church in Birmingham, Alabama.

These people and more made it possible for Jesse Jackson to achieve all that he had as an African American. He told the audience that it was a better day in this country but that much remained to be done. Jackson described the country as a big quilt. "America is not a blanket from one thread, one color, one cloth. When I was a child in South Carolina and Momma couldn't afford a blanket she didn't complain and we didn't freeze. Instead, she took pieces of old cloth...only patches, barely enough to shine your shoes with. But they didn't stay that way long. With sturdy hands and a strong cord, she sewed them together in a quilt, a thing of power, beauty, and culture."

Jesse Jackson was saying that this is how the United States should be. It should be like one big quilt, made up of different fabrics and colors—something of beauty for all to enjoy.

He went on to point out how different groups of people in this country should have a larger patch of the quilt. There should be a big patch for poor farmers who were losing their farms, he said. A patch was needed for students who did not have enough money to go to college. Then there was the patch needed for parents who could not afford after-school programs for their children. All these and many more people deserve a better chance in life, he said.

Michael Dukakis captured the audience with his acceptance speech at the convention. But the excitement in the hall could not be compared to what had taken place the night before when Jackson had spoken.

The television ratings for that week showed an interesting fact. If all the major television stations had not been showing the convention at the same time, Jackson's speech would have been the highest-rated show of the year. *The Cosby Show*, which was the highest-rated program during the period, had drawn a 35 percent rating of the television audience that week. Jackson's speech attracted 48 percent.

A *New York Times* editorial said of him the following day:

> Jesse Jackson did not win the Democratic nomination but he came far closer than any black ever. In the process, he made himself a hero to many, but that is only half the story.
>
> His success depends on much more than his own extraordinary skills. It reflects two dramatic decades in which blacks have deepened and broadened their political consciousness and involvement. His success is a triumph, also, for history...no matter what happens in this or future campaigns he has made Presidential politics a forum for civil rights issues.

THE COMING TOGETHER OF FAMILY

> **When people come together, flowers always flourish and the air is rich with the aroma of a new spring.**
>
> **JESSE JACKSON**

The morning after the Democratic National Convention, Jesse Jackson called together the people who had supported him. It was a kind of where-do-we-go-from-here meeting. Jackson also wanted his followers to know that he was in good spirits even though he had not won the nomination.

Before speaking to the group, Jackson asked one of his aides to introduce some special guests he had invited. The guests turned out to be the new Democratic candidate for president, Michael Dukakis, and his running mate for vice president, Texas Senator Lloyd Bentsen. Their wives were also there.

Jackson's people gave the guests a warm welcome. Some of them shouted, "Duke, Duke," as had been done the night before when Dukakis was named as the party's choice. Dukakis's response to the crowd was, "We need you. This nation needs you. We can't win without you."

Afterward, Bentsen spoke. He offered words of praise for Jackson's leadership in the Democratic party. Then there was loud applause for Jackson. The guests left after that. It was then family time, so to speak.

Jackson loosened his tie and became more casual. He outlined what he felt had been accomplished by his being a candidate. He told of the great increase in voter registration among minority groups. And he told of the ways he had helped shape the platform, and the future direction of the Democratic party.

Some were still feeling bad over his not winning the nomination. But Jackson asked them to remember what Fannie Lou Hamer and the Mississippi Freedom Democratic Party had experienced at the 1964 convention in Atlantic City. "If there's some hurt here today, some pain, remember Atlantic City, 1964," he said. "We couldn't even get in the hall then. We've come too far to turn back now, so let's keep going."

Jesse Jackson kept on going. In the words of the old black spiritual he was "not letting anybody turn him 'round." Operating from his PUSH headquarters, he continued to be a major spokesperson for blacks in this country and abroad.

On July 13, 1989, Jackson was awarded the NAACP's Spingarn Medal at its 80th convention. The Spingarn Medal came a month after Coretta Scott King called Jackson "our leader." She even declared him the heir to the tradition that her husband, Martin Luther King, Jr., had left behind. This occurred during the 18th annual convention of Operation PUSH. There had been years of mixed feelings between Jackson and some of the older civil rights leaders connected to the SCLC, such as Coretta Scott King and Benjamin Hooks, head of the NAACP. But now Coretta Scott King's comment and the Spingarn Medal were seen as acts of peace. Mary Frances Berry, a member of the United States Commission on Civil Rights, described the two events as "the coming together of family."

The medal that Jackson received was named after Joel E. Spingarn who helped establish the NAACP and later served as president of the organization. Spingarn had also founded a publishing company and taught at Harvard University. He had allowed great thinkers of the day such as W. E. B. Du Bois to use his home for special gatherings. Other recipients of the award include King, entertainer Bill Cosby, and James Weldon Johnson who wrote the Black National Anthem.

That same year, the Jackson family moved to Washington, D.C., along with the Rainbow Coalition office. The move raised the question of whether Jackson would run for mayor of the nation's capital, but by 1990 he had said he wouldn't.

After the 1988 election, Jesse Jackson spoke out for change in this country as much as ever. He continued to be a champion for the poor and oppressed throughout the world. In the summer of 1989 he traveled to New York to support hospital union workers of the city who were staging a major strike. Then he returned the following month to support telephone company workers in a protest against their company.

On June 30, 1989, a ceremony was held at the White House in Washington, D.C. It was the 25th anniversary of the 1964 Civil Rights Act.

Jesse Jackson and Rosa Parks were among the civil rights leaders who were there. President Bush spoke to the audience. He said that the government would "enforce civil rights laws." He added that his administration would not tolerate any discrimination.

Jesse and the civil rights leaders felt that the president's remarks did not go far enough. They were especially disturbed over some recent decisions made by the U.S. Supreme Court. During the month of June alone, there had been four major decisions made by the Court that made it harder for someone to file a discrimination suit. The decisions also made it harder to win a case and made it easier for a discrimination case to be thrown out of the courts. Rules that helped women and minorities get jobs they were once locked out of were being dismissed. All of this was seen as a major setback to the cause of civil rights.

Why were so many rollbacks to civil rights legislation taking place? It was because there were many judges on the Supreme Court who were conservative in their thinking. These conservative judges had been named to the Court during the administration of President Reagan. Their appointments had worried civil rights leaders when they first took place. They feared that these judges, whose ideas and thinking were not liberal, might slow down progress for the causes of minorities. And this was exactly what had started to happen.

So the civil rights leaders did not want to go to the White House for just a celebration. They wanted action. They called on the president to address the matter of the setbacks. They wanted him to question what the Supreme Court had done. And they wanted him to come up with new laws that would turn the Court's actions around.

Only days earlier, the president had announced plans to offer such legislation against a decision made by the courts that said flag burning was not illegal. There were cries from the public who thought it was an outrage that the flag could be burned. In reply, the president decided to redress the Court's decision on flag burning by making new laws.

At the Washington gathering, Jesse Jackson said, "The fact is that we all find burning the flag repugnant. We find burning crosses repugnant," he added. He was referring to some Ku Klux Klan activities. "But they have been burning crosses longer than they have been burning flags and there has been no rush for a constitutional amendment to stop the burning of crosses. . . . We cry out to the president for legislative remedy."

Jesse Jackson congratulates future New York mayor David Dinkins on winning the Democratic primary.

Support for a study of the Court's action came from some representatives in Washington. Democratic Senators Edward Kennedy and Howard Metzenbaum and Republican Senator James Jeffords introduced a bill to address the Court's recent rulings on civil rights legislation. They wanted new laws that would help women and minorities in job discrimination cases. Such laws, if passed, would reverse, the recent Supreme Court decisions.

Senator Kennedy agreed with Jackson and other black leaders. He said, "The Supreme Court's recent decisions are serious setbacks for civil rights, especially in the area of job discrimination." He said that Congress was working on repairing what is viewed by many as damage.

THE COMING TOGETHER OF FAMILY **119**

On August 26, 1989, the NAACP led a protest of these civil rights setbacks. More than 5,000 civil rights demonstrators, including Jesse Jackson, walked in the Silent March on Washington. The march, which was silent except for the sound of muffled drums, was patterned after the one held in 1917. At that time, W. E. B. Du Bois had led 8,000 people up Fifth Avenue in New York City to protest the lynchings and segregation that took place during that period. At the first Silent March, all the men wore black; the women and children wore white. The same style was repeated for the Silent March of 1989.

Jesse Louis Jackson spoke at the march. He said that "African-Americans, poor Americans, and others have to exercise their political power to stem the tide of the current court retreat."

Jackson added that the civil rights setbacks were not just about race "but about workers, female heads of households, and Americans who can't afford health care". He called on all Americans to lift their voices against the Supreme Court actions against civil rights.

Jackson is not loved by everyone. Yet millions of people respect him for his accomplishments. All that he has achieved makes him a role model for young people in America. For the left-outs, the people still struggling for their rightful place and share in the wealth of this country, Jesse Jackson is a symbol of hope. Because of the distance he has come—from child of the segregated South—to African-American presidential candidate of the nation, hope is alive. Hope is alive with possibilities for the left-outs that a new quilt of America is being woven. And as Jackson has suggested, in this new quilt, there will be larger patches for them. There is hope also that among their group, there may even be some future weavers—weavers, like Jesse Jackson.

Timetable of Events in the Life of
Jesse Jackson

Oct. 8, 1941	Born in Greenville, South Carolina
1945	Adopted by Charles Henry Jackson
1959	Enters University of Illinois
1960	Transfers to North Carolina Agricultural and Technical State University (North Carolina A & T)
1962	Marries Jacqueline Lavinia Brown; they will have six children: Santita; Jesse Louis, Jr.; Jonathan; Luther; Yusef; and Jacqueline
1963	Graduates from North Carolina Agricultural and Technical College; enrolls in Chicago Theological Seminary
1966	Leads march from Soldier Field to City Hall in Chicago with Martin Luther King, Jr.; heads Southern Christian Leadership Conference's program Operation Breadbasket in Chicago
1970	Organizes first Black Expo, held in Chicago
1971	Organizes People United to Serve Humanity (PUSH); runs for mayor of Chicago
1974	Leads march on Washington, D.C., demanding jobs for the poor
1983–84	Runs for Democratic party's nomination for president of the United States
1987–88	Makes second run for Democratic party's nomination for president
1989	Awarded NAACP's Spingarn Medal

SUGGESTED READING

Branch, Tayler. *Parting the Waters: America in the King Years, 1954–63*. New York: Simon and Schuster, 1988.

*Chaplik, Dorothy. *Up With Hope*. Minneapolis: Dillon Press, 1986.

Collins, Sheila D. *The Rainbow Challenge*. New York: Monthly Review Press, 1981.

*Halliburton, Warren. *The Picture Life of Jesse Jackson*. New York: Franklin Watts, 1984.

*Hatch, Roger D., and Frank E. Watkins, eds. *Straight from the Heart (Essays by Jesse Jackson)*. Philadelphia: Fortress Press, 1987.

*Kosof, Anna. *Jesse Jackson*. New York: Franklin Watts, 1987.

*McKissack, Patricia. *Jesse Jackson: Keep Hope Alive*. New York: Scholastic, 1989.

Morris, Aldon. *Origins of the Civil Rights Movement*. New York: The Free Press, 1984.

Reed, Adolph L., Jr. *The Jesse Jackson Pheonomenon*. New Haven: Yale University Press, 1986.

Reynolds, Barbara A. *Jesse Jackson: The Man, The Movement, The Myth*. Chicago: Nelson-Hill Publishers, 1975.

Stone, Eddie. *Jesse Jackson*. Los Angeles: Holloway House, 1979.

Walker, Wyatt Tee. *Road to Damascus*. New York: Martin Luther King Fellows Press, 1985.

Williams, Juan. *Eyes on the Prize: America's Civil Rights Years 1954–1965*. New York: Viking Penguin, 1987.

*Readers of *Jesse Jackson: Still Fighting for the Dream* will find these books particularly readable.

SOURCES

BOOKS

Branch, Taylor. *Parting the Waters: America in the King Years, 1954–63*. New York: Simon and Schuster, 1988.

Chaplik, Dorothy. *Up With Hope*. Minneapolis: Dillon Press, 1986.

Collins, Sheila D. *The Rainbow Challenge*. New York: Monthly Review Press, 1981.

Faw, Bob and Nancy Shelton. *Thunder in America*. Austin: Texas Monthly, 1986.

Halliburton, Warren. *The Picture Life of Jesse Jackson*. New York: Franklin Watts, 1984.

Haskins, James and Kathleen Benson. *The 60s Reader*. New York: Viking, 1988.

Hatch, Roger D. and Frank E. Watkins, eds. *Straight from the Heart (Essays by Jesse Jackson)*. Philadelphia: Fortress Press, 1987.

Kosof, Anna. *Jesse Jackson*. New York: Franklin Watts, 1987.

McKissack, Patricia. *Jesse Jackson: Keep Hope Alive*. New York: Scholastic, Inc., 1989.

Morris, Aldon. *Origins of the Civil Rights Movement*. New York: The Free Press, 1984.

Reed, Adolph L., Jr. *The Jesse Jackson Phenomenon*. New Haven: Yale University Press, 1986.

Reynolds, Barbara A. *Jesse Jackson: The Man, The Movement, The Myth*. Chicago: Nelson-Hill Publishers, 1975.

Stone, Eddie. *Jesse Jackson*. Los Angeles: Holloway House, 1979.

Walker, Wyatt Tee. *Road to Damascus*. New York: Martin Luther King Fellows Press, 1985.

Williams, Juan. *Eyes on the Prize: America's Civil Rights Years 1954–1965*. New York: Viking, 1987.

MAGAZINE ARTICLES

"Black and White: How Integrated Is America?" *Newsweek*, March 7, 1988.

"Can Jesse Win?" *Ebony*, March 1988.

"A History of Controversy." *Newsweek*, March 21, 1988.

"I'm Not Angry; We'll Keep the Dream Alive." *USA Today*, August 13, 1988.

Edwards, Audrey. "Winning with Jesse." *Essence*, July 1984.

"Jackson's Message." *Newsweek*, March 21, 1988, p. 23.

Klein, Joe. "Dealing with Jesse." *New York Magazine*, March 21, 1988, p. 16.

Klein, Joe. "Jesse Jackson for President." *New York Magazine*, April 11, 1988, p. 29.

"Proud to be Jacksons." *Newsweek*, August 1, 1988.

Purnick, Joyce and Michael Oreskes. "Jesse Jackson Aims for the Mainstream." *New York Times Magazine*, March 30, 1988, p. 3.

"Taking Jesse Seriously." *Time*, April 11, 1988.

"The Dream Then and Now." *Life*, Spring 1988.

"The New Age of Jackson." *U.S. News and World Report*, March 14, 1988.

"The Jackson Problem." *Time*, December 12, 1988.

"Win, Jesse, Win." *Time*, April 4, 1988.

NEWSPAPER ARTICLES

Amsterdam News: January 7, 1989; April 15, 1989.

London Times: May 27, 1989.

New York Post: March 30, 1988.

New York Newsday: April 6, 1988.

New York Times: April 11, 1988; April 16, 1988; April 19, 1988; June 12, 1988; June 28, 1988; July 1, 1988; July 20; 1988; July 22, 1988; January 30, 1989; May 1, 1989; June 3, 1989; June 7, 1989; June 17, 1989.

The Star Ledger: July 20, 1988.

Village Voice: March 8, 1988; April 12, 1988.

Wall Street Journal: July 20, 1988.

INDEX

About the Author

Brenda Wilkinson is the author of four young adult novels. She was born and raised in Georgia and now resides in New York with her two daughters, Kim and Lori. She is currently working on her fifth novel, a contemporary story of young African Americans growing up in the inner city. *Jesse Jackson* is her first biography.